Stena Line
The Fleet Book

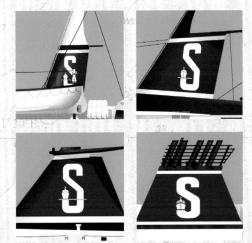

ISBN 978-1-911268-44-4
Produced and designed by Marc-Antoine Bombail & Miles Cowsill
Ship illustrations: ©Marc-Antoine Bombail (www.mab-creations.ch)

Published by Ferry Publications trading as Lily Publications Ltd
PO Box 33, Ramsey, Isle of Man, British Isles, IM99 4LP
Tel: +44 (0)1624 898 446

Printed and bound by Gomer Press Ltd., Wales, UK • +44 (0)1559 362 371 • © 2020 Ferry Publications trading as Lily Publications Ltd
Published: November 2020

Ferry
Publications

Contents

Publishers Note: *With the extensive number of ships that have been chartered by Stena Line or Stena Ro Ro, this book does not claim or set out to include all the ships that have operated with the company since 1962. The book does not include the bulk cargo operations.*

Above: The Skagen II.
Left: Aerial view of the Stena Empereur.

Introduction

Skagen Harbour in 1963.

N ow nearing six decades of operation, Stena Line is one of the most admired names in the ferry industry, constantly in the forefront of innovation in modern ferry development. Primarily known as a Scandinavian ferry operator until the 1990s, today the company is the largest ferry operator in Europe, operating on 19 different routes criss-crossing the Baltic Sea, Scandinavia, North Sea and Irish Sea as well as being one of the biggest in the world. Owned by the Olsson family, Stena Line continues to stress its core value of care: 'care for customers, care for resources and care for each other'.

As a company Stena have long enjoyed a an excellent reputation for their employment practices and harmonious labour relations, with a business ethic described by CEO Dan Sten Olsson as 'capitalism with a conscience'. Change and innovation can be a daunting task but with Stena Line actively encouraging every employee to contribute ideas, no matter how small, this strategy has proved productive. Over 300 improvement projects have been completed over the last decade on both the technical side and in the promotion of in-house efficiency enabling the company to meet the changing needs whilst at the same time creating a sense of corporate bond within its employees. On the wider front Stena Line have been voted multiple winners of both 'Best Ferry Company' and 'World's Leading Ferry Operator'.

In keeping with Sweden being ranked as one of the most sustainable countries in the world the company is very environmentally conscious and fully pro-active in its efforts to operate in a sustainable way. Indeed, it was as long ago as 1990 when Stena's Kiel service ferries were first connected to shore power (known today as 'cold ironing') at Göteborg in order to reduce their CO_2 emissions whilst in port. The corporate vision which is writ large on the sides of their ferries 'Connecting Europe for a Sustainable Future' is therefore not a mere idle boast but ingrained in all their practices, with the company being awarded 'Sustainable Ship Operator of the Year' as a result of their efforts.

The origins of the Stena operation can be traced back to 1939 when Sten Allan Olsson, having cut his 'entrepreneurial teeth' working for a company trading in recycling metals based in Göteborg for the shipbuilding industry, started up his own business. By the end of the Second World War this had developed into a thriving operation with small profits being made. It wasn't until late 1946 that he purchased his first ship, an ex-Norwegian whaler which he converted into a three masted schooner, named after his son Dan. Encouraged by his business success he began to invest in a number of second hand coastal ships mainly carrying scrap metal. He was noted for his pragmatism, adept in both buying vessels cheaply and then selling at a premium.

Sten Olsson's Recycling Metals Office, Göteborg, late 1940s.

It wasn't until 1962 that Olsson ventured into passenger shipping when Stena AB was incorporated, its title being an amalgam of his forename and the first letter of his second. He had been convinced of the viability of day shopping excursions between Göteborg and Skagen in Northern Denmark, where low food prices and duty-free shopping onboard combined with equally low fares would become the recipe for the company's success. Keen to attract the Danes as well he astutely had the funnels of his ships painted in the Danish national colours of red and white. Today, the funnel mark with its angular 'S' and ship sailing on its tail is regarded as a mark of quality and dependability throughout the shipping world.

This title offers a detailed account of the history of this famous and successful Swedish company with descriptions and illustrations of the many outstanding ferries which have served Stena Line, relating how each in turn has played their part in making the company that we know today.

From the outset Stena Line had developed a close relationship with Knud E. Hansen A/S who

Right: The first Stena Germanica.

in turn designed the vast majority of their ferries during the ensuing decades, with architect Robert Tillberg producing most of the stunning interiors, the like of which had never been seen before. The glitzy Internal décor with its extensive use of polished brass, marble, chandeliers and festoon blinds gave passengers an impression of international hospitality comfort, juxtaposed alongside lavish retail outlets driving the on-board sale of tax-free goods. This was exemplified in their futuristic looking *Stena Germanica* (1967) which opened Stena's Göteborg-Kiel service setting new standards in ferry passenger comfort, heralding Stena Line as a serious and substantial player within the European ferry business. As traffic demands rapidly changed more routes opened (as well as closed) with vessels often sold after only a few years (at a profit of course!) having almost immediately become too small for the traffic on offer.

Olsson's shipbuilding strategy was not to restrict himself to local Scandinavian shipyards but to widen the search as to where he would get the best value for money. Making multiple orders, for example, as in the early 1970s when ordering four large ferries from Yugoslavian shipyards for the Göteborg-Kiel and Göteborg-Frederikshavn services and driving

a hard bargain in the process has continued to pay dividends right through to today. One upshot being that within two years of entering service traffic demands meant the Frederikshavn pair had to be 'jumboized' in order to create a second freight deck, now a common but cost effective practice.

Consolidation and further growth continued throughout the 1970's and into the 1980s with multiple orders for passenger/vehicle ferries and freighters, not just for Stena's routes but also for charter or sale. However, the 1980s era was more noted for the industrial unrest across Europe with the day ferries for the Frederikshavn route, *Stena Danica* (still in service today) and *Stena Jutlandica*, being delivered in 1983 over a year late from their Dunkerque shipbuilder. Similarly, four other ferries under construction became victims of the prolonged strikes in the Polish shipyards, with the *Stena Germanica* and *Stena Scandinavica* not entering service until 1987 and 1988 respectively, some four years late. The order for the other two vessels was cancelled.

As the 1990s approached, Stena Line were in an expansive mode position with acquisitions in the North America (local restrictive practices making the venture short-lived), Netherlands, UK, and Poland, with the intention of transforming Stena Line from a Scandinavian operator into a 'global leader' and bringing their much vaunted Stena Travel Concept to a much wider audience. Whilst the purchase of the British ferry operator Sealink British Ferries may have been viewed as an over-costly exercise and less than successful on the English Channel services, Stena Line today are now a dominant player on both the North Sea and Irish Sea. This acquisition effectively doubled Stena Line's size and made it into one of the largest shipping companies in the world.

The introduction to the UK of the HSS (High-speed Sea Service) in 1996 was a public sensation

with its highly advanced design and passenger layouts. However, things did not turn out quite as planned, as these fuel thirsty craft became victims of both rising prices and changing business dynamics requiring a more balanced mix of freight and car traffic all year round. But what innovation! Stena's HSS concept put new life back into travelling and somehow with its final demise towards the end of 2014 the ferry world seemed a little less exciting.

The closing years of the 20th century would also see the introduction of the ro-pax *Stena Jutlandica* (1996) on the Göteborg-Frederikshavn service and more new builds in the shape of the Stena4Runner class freight ships. The *Jutlandica's* success was followed by the construction of four SeaSpacer class ro-pax vessels (two for Harwich with the other two immediately sold on) spawning a boom in such vessels being operated across the Stena network. Today, it is now the world of

Stena Germanica *(1987) and* Stena Danica *(1983)*.

One of the Stena Superfast *vessels superimposed in front of Belfast City Hall.*

the giant ro-pax, epitomised in the superb 63,600gt vessels *Stena Hollandica* and *Stena Britannica* which operate from Hoek van Holland to Harwich, offering not just exceptional passenger comforts but also in their ability to accommodate 5,500 lane metres of lorry traffic. Further expansion would come for Stena Line in 2012 when they seized the opportunity to acquire cross-Baltic ferry services involving Sweden, Germany and Latvia, as well as two more routes on the Irish Sea to Belfast.

Stena Line's success over the years has been largely achieved through their willingness to modify routes according to demand, whilst at the same time continuing the process of introducing new vessels. Their ability to acquire tonnage from other operators and mould them into highly efficient and successful units (e.g. *Stena Superfast VII* and *Stena Superfast VIII* on the Cairnryan to Belfast service) continues to be one of their strengths. Alongside this is the judicious

upgrading of their existing tonnage in making it fit for the challenges ahead; the longevity of the *Stena Danica* (1983) which operates on their Göteborg–Frederikshavn service is a prime example. More recently the *Stena Europe* was sent to the Gemak Shipyard in Tuzla, Turkey in 2019 for 'life extension' work which will keep her in frontline service well beyond her 40th birthday in 2021.

In 2015 in their quest to use alternative fuels with the potential to limit noxious emissions, the *Stena Germanica* became the world's first 'dual fuel' ferry using both methanol and diesel; methanol being deemed to have the potential to limit sulphur emissions almost to zero as well as to significantly reduce those for nitrous oxide. After five years' service the results are encouraging, though at present no other members of the Stena Line fleet have been so treated.

Stena Line is not just not just about Investment in ferries, it is also about investment in its port infrastructures. For example, the Port of Holyhead has gone completely 'green' which included the installation of solar panels installed on the roofs of the terminal buildings providing the port with 100% green energy. Equally, Stena Line transformed their North Channel services with the opening of an impressive new Loch Ryan port just north of Cairnryan in 2011. This £200m major investment also involved working with the port authorities at Belfast to further enhance the facilities there for both the Loch Ryan and Birkenhead services. As Dan Sten Olsson, chairman of Stena AB, commented at the time, 'When Stena invests in infrastructure on this scale it is with a view of recouping the cost over the next half century. In turn this safeguards the ferry link between Scotland and Northern Ireland for the next generations to come'. This is in sharp contrast in a world where making profits in the short term is the only aim. Stena's approach is different, it stands out and is far superior. Stena vision indeed!

In the pre Covid-19 world Stena Line had over 5,000 employees with a turnover income of around SEK 125,000 million (£11,700 million). Over 7.5 million passengers travelled on their 40 vessels (including two on slot charters) together with 2.1 million trucks and 1.7 million cars on their routes across Northern Europe waters. However, the rapid spread of the virulent Covid-19 coronavirus strain during 2020 has had a devastating effect, bringing unprecedented challenges. None more so than on the transport and travel industries, with ferries, cruise ships and aircraft laid up and operators facing major financial difficulties. Stena Line has not been immune from this and has experienced a significant decline in passenger and freight volumes across all its European routes, resulting in having to either furlough employees or make them redundant.

The delivery to Stena Line in 2019/2020 of three E-Flexer ferries ('E' for efficiency) from the Weihai Shipyard in China for service on the Irish Sea marked the culmination of six years of planning to improve efficiency, environmental performance and operating flexibility in ferry operation. The design work for the E-Flexers was trusted to Finnish Naval Architects Deltamarin in conjunction with Stena Ro-Ro and Stena Teknik, whilst the interiors are in the hands of Swedish Company, Figura Arkitekter. Although constructed in China, over 60% of the total components being installed are of European manufacture.

It is a major investment and the entry of the *Stena Estrid* (Holyhead–Dublin), *Stena Edda* and *Stena Embla* (Birkenhead–Belfast) will eventually be followed by two (or possibly four) others for their Baltic services. The design has what is referred to as 'Stenability' allowing for future modifications and configurations on a cost-efficient basis.

With the E-Flexer, Stena has come up with a ferry that is incredibly efficient, flexible and future proof and have most certainly achieved high quality at a very good price. This design is likely to be a successful series of vessels, with some being chartered to other ferry operators and modified during construction to meet their needs.

Stena's vision supported by its undoubted expertise, understanding of the market, flair and financial shrewdness, backed by a willingness to invest long term, is once again showing the way forward. More great things are promised to come including their advanced, fully-electric ferry *Stena Elektra*, which they hope will be in service before this decade is out.

John Bryant
November 2020

Stena Elektra.

The Stena Line Story

The story of Stena Line can be traced back to 1939 when Sten Allan Olsson from Sweden formed a trading company. By 1946 this had developed into a scrap metal and manufacturing company and, with profits made, it was decided to venture into shipping. Until 1962 the company operated small coasters, but in that year Sten formed Stena AB (taking his Christian name and the initial of his second name) and moved into passenger shipping, taking over Skagenlinjen AB and operating small passenger ships between Sweden and Denmark on the Göteborg–Skagen (and later Frederikshavn) and Malmö–Kalstrup routes. The ships were painted white with the familiar 'S' symbol on the red funnel – Stena Line was born.

The following year two car ferries – named the *Stena Danica* and *Stena Nordica* – were ordered from the shipyard at Le Trait in France. The plan was to operate the ships between Göteborg and Frederikshavn but after the *Stena Danica* had entered

Opposite page: Sten A. Olsson.

Below: A busy 1960s scene at Skagen.

Right: The second Stena Danica *at Frederikshavn.*

Below: The Stena Germanica *and* Stena Britannica *in port.*

Opposite: The first Stena Danica *departing Göteborg.*

service in 1965 it was found that traffic was not building up as much as was hoped, and so the second ship went straight to a new service between Tilbury and Calais, marketed as 'The Londoner'. This service was a moderate success but it was decided that the ship was too big and at the end of the summer season she was offered for sale. In the end she was not sold but instead chartered to British Rail to operate on their Stranraer–Larne route, where she remained until 1973. The Tilbury–Calais service resumed the following year but with the smaller *Prinsessan Christina*, chartered from rival operator Sessan Line.

Det finns två sätt
att köra bil snabbt till kontinenten.

Stena Line från Göteborg.

Turlista och prislista t o m 31/12 1970   Göteborg—Danmark (Frederikshavn) Göteborg—Tyskland (Kiel)

In 1967 a new service to Kiel in North Germany was launched and a new ship – the Langesund-built *Stena Germanica* – was constructed for this route. A new, larger *Stena Danica* was delivered in 1969, replacing the older ship after only four years' service. By this time most of the coasters and small passenger vessels had been disposed of by the company.

The 1970s

in 1970 no less than four vessels were ordered from the yard at Trogir, Yugoslavia (now Croatia). Two were destined for the Göteborg–Frederikshavn route to replace the almost brand-new *Stena Danica,* whilst the other two were sold before delivery to Rederi `AB Gotland at a good profit, a typical Stena move which became very apparent with their trading over the next decades. The third *Stena Danica* and running mate *Stena Jutlandica* were delivered in 1974, but by 1977 they too were considered too small and were enlarged to increase vehicle capacity. Previously, on the Göteborg–Kiel route the *Stena Olympica* had entered service in 1972, the year of the Munich Olympics with its running mate, the *Stena Scandinavica* entering service in 1973, both also having been built in Yugoslavia at Kraljevia. The following year four ferries of a then-unusual boxy design were delivered from Bremerhaven. The *Stena Nordica*, *Stena Normandica*, *Stena Nautica*, and *Stena Atlantica* were not acquired for Stena Line service but for the charter market – and all had very productive careers offering high capacity to the rapidly growing car and lorry ferry market both in Europe and worldwide.

Whilst the purchase of passenger ships purely for charter was not repeated, in the 12-driver freight ferry market Stena has been a market leader. Although not operating many such routes themselves at the time, Stena ships and former Stena ships can be found all over the world on routes where the main traffic is trailers and containers on trailers. During the 1970s and early 1980s a bewildering array of ships was launched, with some given Stena names, and some given other names if the charter deal had been agreed before the launch. Most were sister ships, in several classes. The first examples were the 1971–72 built *Stubbenkammer* (for Deutsche Reichsbahn), *Anderida* (for British Rail) and *Stena Trailer* (which also went to British Rail as their *Dalriada* after delivery). Between 1974 and 1977 came the 'Seaporter' class – the *Bison*, *Buffalo*, *Union Melbourne*, *Stena Tender*, *Stena Topper*, and *Stena Timer*. Many of these ships operated for Pandoro and later P&O Irish Sea and remained in service until the closure of the Fleetwood to Larne service in 2010, then operated by Stena Line.

Then in 1977 and 1978 came the 11-strong Korean-built 'Searunner' class with their distinctive 'oil tanker' style design – the *Alpha Enterprise*, *Atlantic Project*, *Atlantic Prosper*, *Elk*, *Imparca Empress*, *Merzario Ausonia*, *Merzario Espania*, *Norsky*, *Stena Runner*, *Stena Transporter*, and *Tor Felicia*. All have different names now, some were lengthened, some modified to ro-pax format with only the *Sea Partner* (ex-*Stena Partner*, ex-*Stena Transporter*, ex-*Alpha Enterprise*) still in service today.

In 1979 Stena Line launched an Oslo–Frederikshavn route using the former Swedish-Lloyd vessel, the 1966-built *Patricia*, which was renamed the *Stena Saga*.

The handsome Stena Saga.

The 1980s

In 1980 a pooling agreement was reached with rival operator Sessan Line (Rederi AB Goteborg–Frederikshavn Linjen) whereby Stena took over the management of both companies' ships and a co-ordinated service was offered, branded as Stena-Sessan Line. Sessan Line had just taken delivery of a new large ferry for their Göteborg–Frederikshavn service called the *Kronprinsessan Victoria*, which was to prove very useful for Stena Line in the ensuing years.

Stena Line had placed orders for no less than six large ferries – two ships built in Dunkerque, France for the Göteborg–Frederikshavn service to be delivered in 1982 and four night superferries to be built in Gdansk and Gdynia, Poland, to be delivered

in 1983–84. Two of the superferries would be used on the Göteborg–Kiel route and the other two chartered out or used to develop new routes. Both deliveries experienced severe delays. The two French-built ships – the *Stena Danica* and *Stena Jutlandica* – were not delivered until 1983 and the situation regarding the Polish-built ships was even worse. Gdansk and Gdynia were the heartland of the Solidarnosc trade union movement, and various industrial disputes were later compounded by the inability of the shipyards to pay for materials. Eventually, Stena Line purchased the first two ferries in their unbuilt state and paid for the necessary materials themselves, reimbursing the shipyards for the work only. The contract for the other two vessels was cancelled, although the shipyard eventually sold both uncompleted hulls. The new *Stena Germanica* did not enter service until 1987 and the second ship, the *Stena Scandinavica,* did not arrive until 1988.

Sessan Line's *Kronprinsessan Victoria* proved a godsend, initially on the Göteborg–Frederikshavn route and then on the German route, with a vehicle deck fitted out with cabins. With the eventual delivery of the Polish ships she was transferred to the Oslo–Frederikshavn route and renamed the *Stena Saga*. Similarly, Sessan Line's Göteborg–Travemunde passenger ferry *Prinsessan Birgitta* was redeployed on Stena's Kiel route and renamed the *Stena Scandinavica*. The Travemunde route, which had a freighter on alternate days, became freight-only.

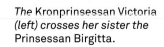

The Kronprinsessan Victoria *(left) crosses her sister the* Prinsessan Birgitta.

The *Lion Prince,*
ex-*Prinsessan Christina.*

Work on Sessan Line's second ship was suspended for a time but she was eventually delivered, in 1982, as the new *Prinsessan Birgitta* and operated initially on the Göteborg–Frederikshavn route, until the following year when she was modified in a similar way to her sister and chartered to British Rail Sealink, where she became the *St Nicholas* on the Harwich–Hook of Holland service.

In 1982 Stena Line AB was renamed Stena AB and became the parent company to the group. Stena-Sessan Linjen AB was renamed Stena Line AB but continued to have outside shareholders and, from 1987, was to be quoted on the Stockholm Stock Exchange. This situation continued until 2001 when the company returned to private ownership.

In 1988 Stena Line purchased Lion Ferry, which operated services between Grenaa in Denmark and Varberg in Sweden: at the same time, Grenaa–Helsingborg service was acquired by DFDS. Later in 1987 Stena Line acquired control of all these services, re-launched the company with a new logo and livery and began giving the ships 'Lion' names. In 1989 they transferred the first *Stena Saga* to the route and renamed her the *Lion Queen*. A Grenaa–Halmstad service was introduced, which lasted until 1999.

During the 1980s both the British Rail ferry line Sealink UK Ltd and the Dutch carrier Stoomvaart Maatschappij Zeeland were

Stena Scandinavica.

privatised. In 1985 control of Sealink was gained by Sea Containers of Bermuda, whilst in 1989 Stena Line acquired the Dutch company which became Stena Line BV. Shortly after this purchase Stena Line began an intensive and sometimes acrimonious campaign to purchase Sealink and eventually, in 1990, the offer was such that the Sea Containers directors could no longer recommend anything other than acceptance to the shareholders. All of Sealink went to Stena, except the ports of Folkestone, Newhaven, and Heysham, and the Isle of Wight operation.

The 1990s

Stena Line entered the 1990s with a fleet which had almost doubled in size following the acquisition of Sealink UK Ltd from Sea Containers. It was a somewhat varied collection of vessels. Sealink had always had trouble in obtaining capital for investment under British Rail ownership, competing with railway-related projects, and things were no better under Sea Containers' ownership, with new ships being only for the Isle of Wight. Initially, the main change was in name from Sealink British Ferries to Sealink Stena

Line, but the livery and logo devised immediately prior to privatisation were retained. Ships gradually received Stena names by the expedient of having the word 'Stena' placed before the previous name (e.g. the *Hengist* became the *Stena Hengist)*. Those ships named after saints received new names, often reviving historic railway ferry names but with the inevitable Stena prefix (e.g. *St Columba* became the *Stena Hibernia*). In 1993 a new livery was devised, still retaining the Sealink logo, but the trading name was changed to Stena Sealink Line. In 1996 the branding became 'Stena Line', using a new style that was applied throughout the fleet.

Having acquired Sealink, Stena Line set about updating the fleet. Two ro-pax ferries – the *Stena Challenger* and the *Stena Traveller* – had been ordered from the Fosen Yard in Norway and both were deployed on Sealink routes – the 'Challenger' first on Dover–Dunkerque, then Dover–Calais, and finally on Holyhead–Dublin. The 'Traveller' also served on Holyhead–Dublin, a service Stena introduced to complement the Holyhead–Dun Laoghaire passenger service. The former DSB ferry *Peder Paars* was placed on the Dover–Calais route as the *Stena Invicta*. Then, in 1996, the 1983-built *Stena Jutlandica*, replaced by a new vessel of the same name, joined the route as the *Stena Empereur*. On the

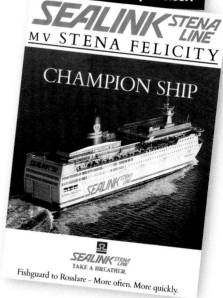

Above: Colourful Stena Line and Stena Sealink brochures from the 1990s.

Left: Stena Challenger.

However, the greatest investment that Stena Line made in its new acquisition was the HSS project. The company started operating fast ferries in 1993 with the punningly titled *Stena SeaLynx*, an Incat 74 metre craft introduced onto the Holyhead–Dun Laoghaire route. Two more similar, but larger, craft were chartered and at various times operated on the Dover–Calais, Newhaven–Dieppe and Fishguard–Rosslare routes The HSS (High-speed Sea Service) was, however, in a different league. At 126 metres long by 40 metres wide, the three largest craft were almost twice as big as the earlier Incats and, with a service speed of 40 knots, about 5 knots faster. They were conceived in the early 1990s and construction began in 1994. The three all went to Stena Line's UK routes: Holyhead–Dun Laoghaire, Belfast–Stranraer, and Harwich–Hook of Holland. With their higher speeds they were able to make more trips than conventional tonnage and faster crossing times were an obvious commercial attraction; in addition, unlike most other fast craft at the time they were able to take premium accompanied freight. Gas turbine power meant a lot of output for a low weight and no need for engine-room staff, but this proved a major problem in the light of escalating oil prices in the next decade, especially for the high-grade fuel used by gas turbines.

Two smaller HSS craft were ordered from Westamarin of Kristiansand, Norway. Carrying 900 passengers, compared with the larger craft's 1,500, the first of these was delivered in 1997 as the *Stena Carisma* and placed on the Göteborg–Frederikshavn service, but whilst the second vessel was in an early stage of construction the builders went into liquidation and all work ended. The partially completed hull of the second vessel was later scrapped.

The HSS 1500 Stena Explorer gets underway at Holyhead.

Harwich–Hook of Holland route, the *St Nicholas* was replaced by the ex-Silja Line vessel *Silvia Regina*, renamed the *Stena Britannica*, then later came the former *Kronprinsessan Victoria*, which became the *Stena Europe*.

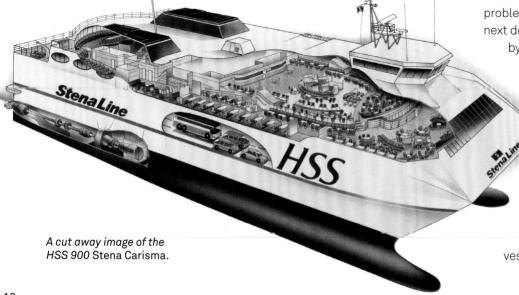

A cut away image of the HSS 900 Stena Carisma.

Stena Europe *departing Fishguard.*

Stena Parisien
(ex-Champs-
Elysées).

The introduction of these revolutionary craft enabled further modernisation of the company's UK-based fleet. The two Harwich–Hook vessels were deployed elsewhere, the Dutch-flagged *Koningin Beatrix* to the Fishguard–Rosslare service and the *Stena Europe* to the Lion Ferry Karlskrona–Gdynia service as the *Lion Europe* (see below). On the Holyhead–Dun Laoghaire route, one ship was retained for the first summer – the *Stena Hibernia*, renamed the *Stena Adventurer* – with the *Stena Cambria* moved to the Dover–Calais service. On the Stranraer–Belfast

route the *Stena Galloway* was sold whilst the *Stena Antrim* was moved to the Newhaven–Dieppe route.

In 1991 Stena Line inaugurated a new service between Southampton and Cherbourg, using the Harwich–Hook of Holland vessel the *St Nicholas*, renamed the *Stena Normandy*. The service ended in December 1996.

In 1992 Stena Line took over the loss-making Newhaven–Dieppe service from French railway company SNCF. The two ships operated – the *Champs Elysees* and *Versailles* (originally the third *Stena*

Danica) – were renamed the *Stena Parisien* and *Stena Londoner* respectively. Stena Line successfully raised standards on this rather 'down at heel' operation although profits continued to be difficult to obtain, especially after the opening of the Channel Tunnel in 1994.

All was not growth, however. In 1991 the Folkestone–Boulogne route was closed and the ships sold, and in 1993 the ro-pax *Stena Challenger* was withdrawn from the Dover–Dunkerque route (although the French-operated train/lorry service continued until early 1996).

In 1998 the Dover and Newhaven operations of P&O European Ferries and Stena Line were merged as P&O Stena Line. Stena Line – which had a 40% share of the new company – contributed the *Stena Cambria, Stena Empereur*, *Stena Fantasia*, *Stena Invicta*, and fast craft *Stena Lynx III*. The 'Invicta' did not operate for the new company and was subsequently sold. The *Stena Cambria* and *Stena Lynx III* operated for one season only at Newhaven, after which the route was closed. The fast craft, which had been renamed the *P&OSL Elite*, was then returned to Stena Line, resuming her previous name, and operating between Fishguard and Rosslare.

In 1995 Stena Line moved into the Baltic with a service between Karlskrona and Gdynia in Poland, under the Lion Ferry name. Initially the route was operated by the 1967-built *Lion Queen* (formerly the *Stena Saga*) but traffic soon outgrew the vessel and the *Stena Europe* joined the route in 1997 as the *Lion Europe*. In 1998 the Lion Ferry brand was dropped and the service was marketed as Stena Line, with the vessel reverting to the name of *Stena Europe*.

On Stena Line's traditional western Scandinavia routes there were less dramatic changes. In 1994, the *Stena Britannica* was transferred to the Oslo–Frederikshavn route and renamed the *Stena Saga*. As previously mentioned, a new Dutch-built ro-pax

Stena Jutlandica was delivered in 1996. The *Stena Nautica,* sister ship of the *Stena Invicta*, was deployed on the Lion Ferry Grenaa–Halmstad route as the *Lion King* between 1995 and 1996, then returned to the route in 1997 as the *Stena Nautica*.

In 1996 Stena ordered seven new ro-ro ships of modern design from Societa Esercizio Cantieri SpA of Viareggio, Italy for delivery in 1997 and 1998. They were known as the Stena 4Runner series and it was planned that some would be chartered to the British Royal Fleet Auxiliary to replace outdated tonnage. Unfortunately, in 1999, and well behind with the orders, the yard went into liquidation. One ship was nearly finished and was moved to another yard for completion and delivery. Two other ships were also in an advanced stage of completion, but it took another four years before they were sold by auction – one going to an Italian company

Stena Transporter, *ex*-Alpha Enterprise.

and completed in another Italian yard and the other purchased by Stena and completed in Croatia. Stena subsequently purchased the Italian-owned vessel and both ships entered service as the *Stena Carrier* and *Stena Freighter* on the Göteborg–Travemunde route in 2004.

In 1997 Stena AB purchased Sweferry AB (trading as Scandlines) from the Swedish State Railways. Renamed Scandlines AB, the company continued to operate separately from Stena Line.

A new century

In 2000 the *Stena Nautica* was again transferred to the Varberg–Grenaa route. During winter 2001–2002 she was rebuilt to heighten her upper vehicle deck and allow the separate loading of vehicle decks; her passenger capacity now reduced.

In 2001 Stena Line upgraded the Holyhead–Dublin route through the charter of the new Italian Visentini Group ro-pax *Stena Forwarder*, replacing

Stena Adventurer.

the *Stena Challenger* which was sold. She in turn was replaced two years later by the even larger *Stena Adventurer*. The ro-pax vessels on the Harwich–Hook of Holland route were also replaced in 2001 with the Spanish-built *Stena Britannica* and *Stena Hollandica*. In typical Stena style, the company actually ordered four ships but sold the first two to Finnlines before they were completed. The previously-operated freighters, with capacity for drivers, inaugurated a new service from Hook of Holland to Killingholme, near Immingham. Good traffic growth led to their replacement by new tonnage in 2006 and 2007. The 2001-built *Stena Britannica*, used on the evening service from the Hook, was replaced in 2003 by a new ship of the same name which gave extra capacity to this busy service. The older ship then joined her two near-sisters with Finnlines.

Stena Line's new route between Karlskrona and Gdynia showed remarkable growth in the few years it had operated and, by 2001, the *Stena Europe* was proving too small. Accordingly, she swapped roles with the *Koningin Beatrix*, operating between Fishguard and Rosslare, this ship being renamed the *Stena Baltica*. Both ships received modifications to increase freight capacity – the *Stena Europe* having the extra cabins that were installed on the car deck 20 years earlier removed before she entered onto the Irish route, and the *Stena Baltica* having rather more complex modifications made in 2005. Additionally, in 2002, a second vessel was placed on the Polish route in the form of the 1992-built *Stena Traveller*. She was replaced in 2004 by the former P&O Irish Sea vessel *European Ambassador*, which was renamed the *Stena Nordica*. In 2007 a third vessel was added to the route in the form of the chartered *Finnarrow* from Finnlines.

Stena Line's joint venture with P&O on the Dover–Calais route came to an end in 2002, when P&O

Stena Navigator passes the Corsewall Lighthouse.

The lengthened Stena Germanica III *(2010, ex-*Stena Hollandica *2001), passes the* Stena Germanica II *(1987), the latter now renamed* Stena Vision.

bought out the Stena Line share. At the same time, Stena Line took over P&O's three-ship Felixstowe–Rotterdam service, moving the UK terminal to Harwich after a few months. A similar arrangement took place on the Irish Sea in 2004, when Stena Line took over P&O's Fleetwood–Larne route and agreed to move their North Channel operation, in due course, from Stranraer to the P&O port of Cairnryan, but this did not take place. Plans for Stena to take over P&O's Liverpool–Dublin service were blocked by the UK Office of Fair Trading on competition grounds, despite alternative services offered by Irish Ferries and Norse Irish Ferries.

In early 2007 Stena Line withdrew the HSS *Stena Discovery* from the Harwich–Hook of Holland service on economic grounds. High fuel costs had combined with a loss of passenger traffic due to the ending of duty-free sales and the growth of low-cost airlines. All traffic, including the carriage of foot passengers, was directed to the ro-pax ships which operated both day and night sailings. Both the *Stena Britannica* and *Stena Hollandica* were lengthened during the first half of the year to bring them to about 240 metres long and additional cabins and other facilities were fitted. The second lengthened ship – the originally smaller *Stena Hollandica* – resumed service in May.

Following the debacle over the original Stena 4Runner ships in the 1990s, Stena ordered three improved versions of the same design from the Dalian shipyard in China. The Stena 4Runner Mark II ships were delivered in 2002 and 2003 and chartered out. New ro-pax ships for the Hook of Holland–Killingholme service (the *Stena Trader* and *Stena Traveller*) were delivered in 2006 and 2007. They replaced the *Stena Searider,* which was sold, and the *Stena Seatrader* which moved to the Irish Sea to provide additional capacity on the Holyhead–Dublin route. It was not until 2011 that two more ships of similar design, the *Stena Transit* and *Stena Transporter* (but each with an additional trailer deck), took over the Killingholme route.

Late in 2006 Stena Line announced the order for two giant ro-pax ferries to be built in the Warnemunde and Wismar yards of Aker Yards (yards now owned by Waden Yards). The new *Stena Britannica* and *Stena Hollandica* would be 240 metres long and provide a staggering 5,500 lane metres for freight, plus another 700 metres for cars. The 63,600t vessels were to be delivered in 2010 replacing the existing ships on the Harwich–Hook route, which would be renamed and moved to the Karlskrona–Gdynia service.

In 2008, with continually rising oil prices, the decision was made to decelerate the two remaining UK HSS services between Holyhead and Dun Laoghaire, and Stranraer and Belfast, and reduce frequencies. In addition, a new terminal was opened at Belfast, nearer the mouth of Belfast Lough, reducing the length of the voyage by several miles. Plans to move to the P&O port at Cairnryan were

The current Stena Hollandica, *built in 2010.*

scrapped due to escalating costs and other options were examined. In the autumn, the *Stena Nordica* was moved from the Karlskrona–Gdynia route to Holyhead–Dublin, replacing the *Stena Seatrader* and enabling four passenger services each way to be operated. In 2009, the Harwich–Rotterdam freight route was reduced to a two-ship service and the smaller *Stena Transporter* laid-up.

A decade of expansion and change

With bunker prices skyrocketing from 2000 and peaking in late 2006, eventually the company decide to withdraw their HSS operations over the next couple of years following the withdrawal of the *Stena Discovery* in 2007, the Belfast link closed in 2011 with the opening of the new terminal at Cairnryan and the seasonal operation between Holyhead and

Dun Laoghaire closed a year later. The *Stena Carisma* remains laid-up at Göteborg, she has not seen service since 2013.

The *Stena Britannica* and *Stena Hollandica* entered service in 2010, and both ships were to prove an overwhelming success with their stylish passenger accommodation and freight capacity for 300 lorries. The transfer of the older ships to the Keil route again brought increased capacity for freight and a more balanced passenger capacity for the link between Sweden and Germany. The former Polish-built ships on the German service were transferred to the now rapidly growing Karlskrona–Gydnia route as the *Stena Spirit* and *Stena Vision*. Further tonnage was later added to route with the *Stena Baltica*, chartered to Stena Line by Brittany Ferries.

In December 2010, Stena Line announced it had acquired the Irish Sea operations

Three Stena ships together at Frederikshavn. Left to right: Stena Saga, Stena Danica *and* Stena Vinga.

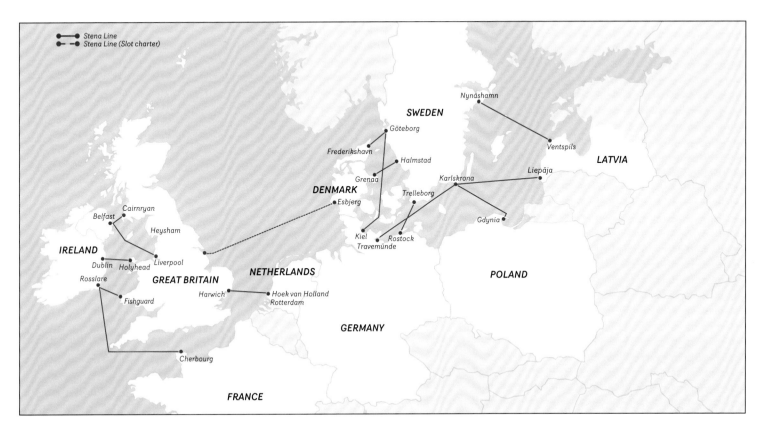

Stena Line passenger routes in 2020.

of DFDS Seaways. The sale included the Belfast to Heysham and Birkenhead routes, two vessels from the Heysham route (*Scotia Seaways* and *Hibernia Seaways*) and two chartered vessels from the Birkenhead route – the *Mersey Seaways* and *Lagan Seaways*. The purchase of this operation allowed the company to take further dominance on the Irish Sea. The Birkenhead route to Belfast rapidly grew, with larger ships and an increased number of ships supporting the route.

In 2011, Stena Line announced that they had chartered two former 'Superfast' ships to operate from their new port of Cairnryan (Loch Ryan) as from November. In another shrewd move to establish their dominance on the North Channel, the former

Superfast VII and *Superfast VIII* were sent for extensive conversion works for their new Cairnryan–Belfast link. The German-built stylish ships replaced three vessels and proved to be very popular on the link; the *Stena Superfast VII* and *Stena Superfast VIII* were later purchased.

A year later, Stena Line acquired five new ferry routes between Sweden and Germany to Latvia, expanding their operations in the Baltic. The expansion into the Baltic increased their presence in both freight and passenger operations. Apart from the purchase of the three routes between Germany and the Baltic States, Stena Line also acquired the vessel *Sassnitz* and the operations on the routes from Trelleborg to Rostock and Sassnitz.

Above: The Stena Estrid *under construction in Weihai, China.*

Below: Stena RoRo acquired the Yamato *from Japan in 2020. She will be adapted to European standards in Greece and will be chartered out during 2021.*

was in response to a request from Stena Line for a new type of ferry which could serve as both a day and overnight ferry. The first of the new ships to enter service was the *Stena Estrid* on the Dublin–Holyhead route in late 2019, followed by the *Stena Edda* for the Belfast–Birkenhead route in March 2020. A further ship in the series, *Stena Embla,* will join the 'Edda' in 2021. Both Brittany Ferries and DFDS took options to acquire these new series of ships for their operations. The French company will operate three of the ships on their Spanish service, entering service between 2020 and 2024. Meanwhile DFDS will employ their ship the *Cote d'Opale* on their Dover–Calais link as from 2021. Stena Line took the option to build two further ferries in the series for delivery in 2024 – it is understood they will operate in the Baltic when they enter operation in 2025.

Again, to be at the forefront of the ferry business, five new next-generation passenger ferries were ordered from China in 2016 for delivery from 2020. The E-Flexer class was designed by Stena Ro-Ro and Deltamarin for use by sister company Stena Line, as well as for long-term charter to other operators. Designed to be environmentally friendly and efficient, the new ferries were also designed to be flexible and to be suitable for numerous routes from short day crossings to overnight services. The E-Flexer project

In February 2020, the company transferred the *Stena Nautica* from Varberg to Halmstad for their link to Grenaa in Denmark, in a move to attract new business from southern Sweden.

Following the *Stena Edda* entering service on the Belfast–Birkenhead, the *Stena Lagan* was sent to Turkey for jumboization. The *Stena Mersey* will follow once the *Stena Embla* is in service. Both former Irish Sea vessels will replace the smaller Visentini ships currently on the Nynäshamn–Ventspils route.

Stena Line today and Covid-19

As 2020 dawned, like so many companies, Stena Line was looking forward to a bright new decade. Covid-19 was to make a major impact on the ferry business in 2020 and the Swedish company were quick to react to the pandemic with their marginal operations, and the Oslo service and the Sassnitz link were closed in March. The company continued their other operations in Europe during the crisis, but with very few passengers on all their links until the late spring; initial freight loadings were to take a downturn, but as the world adapted to the pandemic traffic gradually returned.

Stena Line today is a major international transport and travel services company, and one of the world's largest ferry operators. The ferry business consists of Stena Line AB, which is divided into three business areas: Scandinavia, North Sea, and Irish Sea. Since 2000, the shipping company Scandlines AB has also been a wholly-owned subsidiary of Stena Line.

The route network consists of nineteen strategically-located ferry routes and four ports in Scandinavia and around the UK. The fleet today consists 40 multi-purpose ferries and ro-ro ferries for freight, including some on charter or slot charter.

Stena Line has in total around 5,000 employees, of whom around two-thirds are employed on board. In 2019 Stena Line transported 2.1 million freight units, 1.7 million cars. 7.5 million passengers, with a turnover of fourteen billon Swedish Krona.

Stena Estrid.

The Fleet 1962-2021

Østersøen - 1962 (chartered)

Svendborg Værft / Burmeister & Wain, Denmark, 1954
1,389g / 48.1 x 10.5 m / 700 pass. / 50 cars
Stena Line service: 1962-1963

The first ferry that was chartered by the company. She had her passenger accommodation extended in 1960 and was chartered by Skagen–Göteborg Linien AS. The operation with this vessel was short lived after various problems with this company. Under Sten A. Olsson management she opened Skagen link again and proved the first success story for Stena.

Skagen II - 1963

Oskarshamn Mekaniska Verkstad, Oskarshamn, Sweden, 1924
828g / 54.3 x 9.4 m / Single screw / 12 knots / 470 pass.
Stena service: 1963-1968

Built as the Visby in 1924 for service to the island of Gotland. In 1963 she was sold to Skagenlinjen Rederi AB, Göteborg (Stena AB) for SEK105,000 and renamed Skagen II. Whilst in service on Frederikshaven link in 1964 there was a fire on board which killed three people. She remained with the company until 1966, when she sold for a profit by Stena.

Skagen I - 1963

Burmeister & Wain, Copenhagen, Denmark, 1914
1,325g / 71.1 x 10.4 m / Single screw / 12 knots / 520 pass. / 35 cars
Stena service: 1963-1965

Delivered in April 1914 for the Copenhagen–Rønne, Bornholm service. After various operations in Sweden and Finland for the next fifty years she was chartered in April 1963 to Skagen Line, Göteborg (Stena AB) and re-named Skagen. She was purchased a year later by Stena for SEK 255,000 and in 1965 sold for scrap at a profit of SEK 55,000.

Isefjord - 1963

Aalborg Maskin & Skibsbyggeri, Ålborg, Denmark, 1935
625g / 60.9 x 11.6 m / Twin screw / 12 knots / 500 pass. / 52 cars
Stena service: 1963-1965

Built for the Grenaa–Hundested service in 1935, as one of the first pioneers of car ferry operations in Europe. She was sold in 1963 to Kiel–Nakskov Linien A/S Nakskov, Denmark (A Danish subsidiary of Stena Line). She remained with company for next three years and then sold by Stena for service in Naples. She was sold for scrap in 2008.

Poseidon - 1964

This was the first ship built by Stena Line for their Göteborg–Frederikshavn/Skagen link. Costing some SEK6m, she was to prove highly lucrative for the new company. She was designed by Knud E. Hansen A/S and built in Norway. When the President of the Soviet Union Nikita Kruschev visited Göteborg in 1964 to view the shipbuilding industry, he travelled on the Poseidon.

In June 1964 she entered service on the Göteborg–Frederikshavn/Skagen routes. In the summer of 1966, she was chartered to operate on the Stockholm–Mariehamn service under the name *Jätten Finn*. Sold in 1973 to French interests, she was sold again the following year to L. Remeeuws Bekeer BV, Vlissingen, Holland and chartered to Zeeland Lloyd for a new service between Vlissingen and London. On her first voyage she ran aground near Tower Bridge, London. Later in the year she opened another new link between Vlissingen and Great Yarmouth, then Zeebrugge, but both routes were not successful.

The following year she was sold to German interests and operated in Northern Europe until she was sold again in 2000 to Panamanian interests for service between Gdansk–Baltic–

Kaliningrad as the *Poseidon IV*. Two years later she was sold to Pearl Cruise Line, Colombo, Sri Lanka for service between Colombo and Tuticorin as the *Pearl Cruise II*. She was sold for scrap in 2006.

Ulstein M/V A/S, Ulsteinvik, Norway, 1964
1,358g / 66.5 x 11.9 m / Twin screw / 21 knots / 805 pass.
Stena service: 1964-1972

Afrodite - 1964

D.W Kremer & Son, Elmshorn, Germany, 1964
564g / 42.5 x 8 m / Twin screw / 18 knots / 350 pass.
Stena service: 1964-1971

Built for originally for the Danish-German service of Stena in 1964. After two years' service on various operations with Stena Line, she was chartered out for a number of ship operations in Sweden and Germany before she was sold in 1971. As late as 2015 the ship was still in operation in Sierra Leone.

Wappen - 1964

Blohm & Voss, Hamburg, Germany, 1962
828g / 104 x 15.1 m / Twin screw / 21 knots / 1,800 pass.
Stena service: 1964-1965

Built as the Wappen Von Hamburg in Germany for service between Hamburg–Cuxhaven–Helgoland. In 1963 she was chartered out to Skagenlinjen AB, Göteborg for their Göteborg–Frederikshavn link. The following year she was back in Germany before she was sold to Stena Reederei GmbH and renamed Wappen for the Göteborg–Frederikshavn and Göteborg–Sandefjord services. After only two years she was re-sold by Stena to Hafen Dampschiffart in Germany and renamed Alte Liebe.

Stena Danica - 1965

As early as 1963, Stena's technical department started to draw up designs for two new modern ferries for Danish routes. A contract to build two ferries was signed a year later with the French shipyard Ateliers et Chantiers de la Seine-Maritime, Rouen. When the new ships were introduced the marketing name was changed from Skagenlinjen to Stenalinjen (Stenaline), the concept of Stena Line was not fully introduced until April 1967.

The first ship delivery in 1965 was the *Stena Danica* and she was placed on the Göteborg–Frederikshavn route with two trips in each direction daily. Her sister ship *Stena Nordica* was delivered in June 1965 to operate the Nakskov–Kiel route, however it was eventually decided that she would open a new route between Tilbury and Calais marketed as the 'The Londoner'.

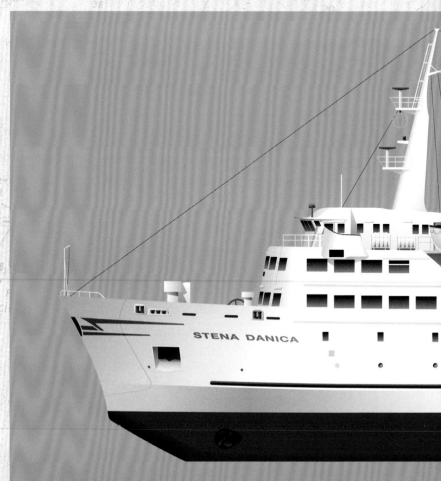

In late 1967 the *Stena Danica* was chartered to Townsend Car Ferries Ltd for their Dover–Zeebrugge route for six months. The *Stena Danica* remained in service with Stena Line until June 1969, before she was sold to the Government of Canada (Ministry of Transport) and renamed *Lucy Maud Montgomery* for service between Cape Tormentine–Port Borden. It is believed she remained in service up until 2010 in South America after her sale in Canada in 1999.

Ateliers et Chantiers de la Seine-Maritime, Le Trait, France, 1965
2,612g / 79.8 x 16.2 m / Twin screw / 17.5 knots
1,000 pass. / 129 cars or 28 lorries, (main deck), 40 cars (side galleries)
Stena service: 1965-1969

TILL DANMARK MED
KOMFORTFÄRJAN
M/S STENA DANICA
Göteborg–Frederikshavn 1965
SKAGENLINJEN REDERI AB

STENA DANICA

STENA DANICA
GÖTEBORG

Stena Nordica - 1965

Ateliers et Chantiers de la Seine-Maritime, Le Trait, France, 1965
2,607g / 79.8 x 16.2 m / Twin screw / 17.5 knots
935 pass. / 85 cars or 28 lorries, (main deck), 40 cars (side galleries)
Stena service: 1965-1973

Delivered in June 1965, the Stena Nordica opened a new link between London and Calais marketed as 'The Londoner'. In January 1966 she was chartered out long-term to the Caledonian Steam Packet Co, Scotland, and re-designed into two classes for her new role. In 1973 she was sold to Naviera Nueva Esparta SA, Venezuela and renamed Santa Ana.

Stena Baltica - 1966

A/S Langesund Mekaniske Verksted, Langesund, Norway, 1966
1,157g / 61.8 x 12.6 m / Twin screw / 15 knots / 580 pass. / 50 cars
Stena service: 1966-1969

Launched in March 1965 and delivered the following year for the Göteborg–Frederikshavn route. In 1969 she was sold to the Caledonian Steam Packet Co Ltd, Scotland. She was renamed the Caledonia and placed on their Ardrossan–Brodick route. After eighteen years of service in Scotland she was sold to Italian interests and renamed Heidi.

Stena Germanica - 1967

In 1964 Stena Line ordered a pair of larger overnight ferries for their operations between Germany and Sweden. The first ship, the *Stena Germanica* was delivered in April 1967. She entered service later in the month on the Göteborg–Kiel service, and was also placed on the Göteborg–Frederikshavn route during peak periods.

Both 'Germanica' and her sister were beautifully designed ships but also very fast with a service speed of 23.5 knots, so they could do the Kiel link in under 12 hours. During 1972, Stena opened another German service between Kiel and Korsör, to make better use of the ship. The early seventies saw various charter work for the *Stena Germanica* including Marseilles–Algiers, Swansea–Cork and also a charter for Shell UK as a

transport vessel between Aberdeen and the Brent field in the North Sea.

In 1979 she was sold to Armatur SA Panama (Corsica Ferries) and renamed the *A Regina*. In 1984 she was chartered to Dominican Ferries for service between Mayaguez and San Pedro de Macoris in the Caribbean. The following year she went at full speed onto a reef and became a wreck at Mona Island, 40 miles west of Puerto Rico.

A/S Langesund Mekaniske Verksted, Langesund, Norway, 1967
5,195g / 110.8 x 18 m / Twin screw / 23.5 knots
1,300 pass. / 220 cars / 15 lorries
Stena service: 1967-1979

"The Londoner"

Continental cruise-a-car
Passenger Ferry

Sails daily
London to Calais
with coach services to

PARIS	3 DAY	2 DAY
Only £6.19.0 return	Mini Holiday in Paris for 2 £9.14.0 per person	Mini Holiday in Calais for 2 £6.2.0 per person
Adult 79/- single Child 79/- return Child 49/- single		

THE LONDONER

STENA BALTICA

S
STENA LINE
THE FRIENDLY LINE

I år har Stena Line två Jätten Finn till Åland från Stockholms city.

Morgonbåten M/S "Stena Finlandica" och lunchbåten M/S "Poseidon"!

JÄTTEN FINN
STENA FINLANDICA

TILL DANMARK – KONTINENTEN MED MODERNA BILFÄRJAN M/S STENA DANICA

Dagligen Göteborg–Frederikshavn från Stenpiren – Danmarkskajen mitt i Göteborg!

STENA DANICA

Stena Britannica - 1967

STENA BRITANNICA

A/S Langesund Mekaniske Verksted, Langesund, Norway, 1967
5,073g / 110.8 x 10.8 m / Twin screw / 23.5 knots / 1,170 pass. / 210 cars
Stena service: 1967-1968

After only a short period on the Frederikshavn–Kiel services she was sold by Stena in 1968 to the State of Alaska renamed Wickersham. In 1974 she was sold to Rederi Ab Sally, Mariehamn, Finland and became the Viking 6. For the next six years she operated various operations in the Baltic. In 1980 she was chartered to Brittany Ferries and became the Goëlo. In 1982 saw her sold to Sol Lines and 1987 she became the Moby Dream, five years later Sardegna Bella for service between Livorno–Olbia. In 2001 she was sold for scrap following an earlier fire in 1998.

Stena Danica - 1969

A.G. Weser Werk Seebeck, Bremerhaven, Germany, 1969
5,537g / 125 x 19.7 m / Twin screw / 22.5 knots / 1,530 pass. / 250 cars
Stena service: 1969-1974

Stena's wonder ship at the time, at her launch she was the biggest and best-appointed day ferry in the world. After only five years on the Göteborg–Frederikshavn route, she was sold to British Columbia Ferries and renamed Queen of Surrey. In 2006 whilst on a voyage between Prince Rupert–Port Hardy, as the now renamed Queen of the North, she ran aground on Gil Island and sank after an hour.

Stena Atlantica - 1972

Lindholmens Varv Ab, Göteborg, Sweden, 1966
7,889g / 141.2 x 21 m / Twin screw / 18 knots / 1,500 pass. / 100 cars
Stena service: 1972-1973

Built as the Saga for the Göteborg–Tilbury (London) service. In 1972 she was acquired by Stena A/B for their Göteborg–Kiel service at a cost of SEK33m and renamed Stena Atlantica. Sold the following year to Finnish interests for SEK43,875m and renamed Finnpartner. Later operated as the Olau Finn. In 1984 she was sold to Minoan Lines and entered service on the Piraeus–Heraklion route as the Festos. She was scrapped in 2003.

Älvpilen - 1972

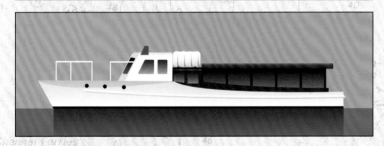

Norrvikens Båtvarv Ab, Vätö, Sweden, 1946
15.8 x 3.4 m / Single screw / 45 pass.
Stena service: 1972-1974

Following the new terminal opening at Göteborg in 1972, Stena Line decided to create additional marketing buzz around its new terminal. The company bought a small harbour boat the Älvpilen (the "river arrow") during the premiere year of the new facilities. They used the boat for guided trips around the harbour to show off their new terminal and the current fleet. The price of the trip included a coffee and a Danish pastry. At the time the Germany-bound ferries pointed downstream in the River Göta, with the Denmark ferries down.

Stena Finlandica - 1972

Howaldtswerke AG, Hamburg, Germany, 1963
2,746g / 91.5 x 14.5 m / Twin screw / 19 knots / 1,500 pass.
Stena service: 1972-1974

Built as the Helgoland in 1963. During her early career she was chartered to Stena Line for various operations and then later purchased by the company in 1972. Renamed Stena Finlandica after a major rebuilding and refurbishment. After various work within the company, she was sold in 1976 for further service in Germany. In 2001 she was sold to South American interests.

Stena Olympica - 1972

The *Stena Olympica* was built in Yugoslavia and delivered in the same year as the summer Olympics in Munich in 1972. Designed by Swedish architects Rolf Carlsson and Hans Nilsson, the interior of the *Stena Olympica* was very spacious and comfortable. The modern stylish onboard accommodation signalled a clear stylistic departure from the former Stena Line ferries, which had generally traditional maritime interiors with wooden surfaces and softer colours. The *Stena Olympica* featured bright colours throughout.

The restaurant deck upstairs was based on Knud E. Hansen's concept of a restaurant in the bow and cafeteria in the stern. The bars onboard had names related to the Olympic Games. She only cost 28 million Swedish kroner in 1972.

After 10 years in traffic, *Stena Olympica* was replaced with larger tonnage. She was then sold to Prince of Fundy Cruises Ltd and used in their summertime route between Portland, Maine and Yarmouth, Nova Scotia as the *Scotia Prince*. In 1986, the ferry was extended and continued on the same route until the operation was discontinued in 2005. For the next six years she was deployed in the Mediterranean and then she was scrapped in Bangladesh after a successful 40-year long career.

Titovo Brodogradiliste, Kraljevica, Yugoslavia, 1972
7,118g / 124.8 x 19.5 m / Twin screw / 22 knots
1,500 pass. / 250 cars
Stena service: 1972-1982

STENA OLYMPICA
GÖTEBORG

Stena Jutlandica - 1973

Brodogradiliste Jozo Lozovina Mosor, Trogir, Yugoslavia, 1973
6,333g / 124.8 x 21.9 m / Twin screw / 22 knots
1,800 pass. / 250 cars
Stena service: 1973-1982

Operated the Göteborg–Frederikshavn route. In 1976 she was jumboized in Holland, with her upper car deck raised by 2.3 meters to allow trailers to use it and sponsons fitted for stability. Became the Bluenose in 1982 then Euroferrys Atlantica in 1999 before being scrapped in 2010.

Stena Scandinavica - 1973

Titovo Brodogradiliste, Kraljevica, Yugoslavia, 1972
7,125g / 124.8 x 19.5 m / Twin screw / 22 knots
1,500 pass. / 250 cars
Stena service: 1973-1978

Sister to the Stena Olympica, she was deployed on the Göteborg–Kiel and also Kiel–Korsör and Göteborg–Frederikshavn routes until sold to Irish Continental Line in 1978 and renamed the Saint Killian, then Saint Killian II. Jumboized in 1981, she was sold to Greece in 1998 becoming the Medina Star. She was scrapped in 2007.

Stena Normandica - 1974

Rickmers Werft, Bremerhaven, Germany, 1974
5,426g / 120.8 x 19.5 m / Twin screw / 20.2 knots / 1,084 pass. / 480 cars
Stena service: 1974-1985

Built in 1974 for Stena Line, she was the first of a series of four ships intended-ed for charter work, all designed and built by Rickmers Werft, Bremerhaven. In 1979, Stena Normandica underwent a long-term charter to Sealink UK. Sold in 1985 and became the St Brendan, then Moby Vincent in 1990.

Stena Nautica - 1974 / Marine Nautica - 1974

Rickmers Werft, Bremerhaven, Germany, 1974
5,537g / 120.8 x 19.5 m / Twin screw / 18 knots
1,200 pass. / 479 cars / 792 lane metres
Stena service: 1974-1981

Second of a series of four ships, she was immediately chartered to Marine Atlantic (Canada) after delivery for a service between North Sydney and Port aux Basques as the Marine Nautica. She was sold to them four years later. In 1986 she was sold to Corsica Ferries and renamed Corsica Marina II (then later Corsica Marina Seconda) for their Livorno–Bastia service.

Stena Atlantica - 1974 / Marine Atlantica - 1975

Rickmers Werft, Bremerhaven, Germany, 1974
5,443g / 120.8 x 19.5 m / Twin screw / 18 knots
1,200 pass. / 479 cars / 792 lane metres
Stena service: 1975-1979

Built in Germany as the third of a series of four sister-ships. After delivery she was immediately chartered to Marine Atlantic (Canada) for a service between North Sydney and Port aux Basques as the Marine Atlantica. She was sold to them in 1979. In 1986, she was sold again, becoming the Corsica Vera, then Sardinia Vera, linking Livorno and Golfo Arranci (Sardinia).

Stena Danica - 1974 / Stena Nordica - 1974

Brodogradiliste Jozo Lozovina Mosor, Trogir, Yugoslavia, 1974
6,333g / 124.8 x 21.9 m / Twin screw / 22 knots / 1,800 pass. / 425 cars
Stena service: 1974-1988, 1992-1996

Built as the Stena Danica she was later renamed Stena Nordica. In 1983 she was chartered to RMT for service between Oostende and Dover. In 1984 she was renamed Stena Nautica. In 1987, she was chartered to SNCF for service between Newhaven–Dieppe as the Versailles and purchased the following year. From 1992 to 1996 Versailles was chartered to Sealink Stena Line as the Stena Londoner. Then she became the SeaFrance Monet on the Dover–Calais route, and in 2000 the Volcan de Tacande.

Stena Nordica - 1975

Rickmers Werft, Bremerhaven, Germany, 1975
5,443g / 120.8 x 19.5 m / Twin screw / 18.5 knots
1,200 pass. / 450 cars / 792 lane metres
Stena service: 1975-1978, 1979-1980, 1980-1981

The last in a series of four ships, the Stena Nordica entered service in November 1975. Between May and November 1976, she was chartered to Marine Atlantic, then again during the summers of 1977-1981. Chartered in 1980 to B&I Line, then later to RMT, who purchased her in 1983 and renamed her Reine Astrid. Became the Moby Kiss in 1997.

Stena Oceanica - 1978

Lindholmens Varv Ab, Göteborg, Sweden, 1967
14,138g / 141.2 x 22.5 m / Twin screw / 18 knots
1,300 pass. / 275 cars / 520 lane metres
Stena service: 1978-1997

Built in 1967 as the Patricia for Southampton–Bilbao service of Swedish Lloyd. Sold to Stena Line in 1978 and renamed the Stena Oceanica (car deck raised by 1.15 metres and deckhouse extended fore and aft). Renamed the Stena Saga in 1979, Lion Queen in 1988, then Crown Princess in 1990. Sold in 1997 in Asia and became the casino ship Putri Bintang.

Stena Baltica - 1978

Oy Wärtsilä Ab, Helsingfors, Finland, 1966
7,586g / 134.4 x 22.5 m / Twin screw / 21 knots / 1,200 pass. / 240 cars
Stena service: 1978-1982

Built as the Finnpartner. During her early career she carried out various charters as well operating on the Helsinki–Nynäshamn / Slite–Karlskrona–Lübeck routes. Renamed Sveaborg in 1969, she was sold to Stena Line in 1978 becoming Stena Baltica. After rebuilding programme by Stena she was chartered to BP for their oil operations in the Shetland Isles. In 1981 sold to Greek interests and renamed the Ialyssos.

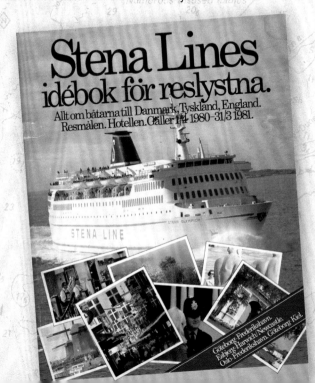

Kronprinsessan Victoria - 1981

The *Kronprinsessan Victoria* entered service between Göteborg and Frederikshavn in April 1981. Soon afterwards, Stena Line AB acquired a majority share ownership in Sessan Linjen. The *Kronprinsessan Victoria* was rebuilt as a day/night ferry and transferred to the Göteborg–Kiel route.

In 1988, *Kronprinsessan Victoria* was renamed *Stena Saga* and transferred to the Oslo–Frederikshavn–Göteborg routes. In 1994 she was transferred

Stena Sessan Line

NR. 2 – 1/7 81

Fartplan og priser 1981

STENA EUROPE

STENA EUROPE

STE

to the Harwich–Hook of Holland route and renamed the *Stena Europe*. In 1997 *Stena Europe* transferred to the Karlskrona–Gdynia route becoming the *Lion Europe*, when she was replaced by *Stena Discovery*. She reverted back to the name *Stena Europe* the following year, when Stena Line dropped the Lion Ferry marketing name.

In November 2008 the *Stena Europe* received an €850,000 refurbishment to its main passenger areas, and in 2019 she was sent to the Gemak Shipyard in Tuzla in Turkey for a major refit. The work undertaken during this refit should see her continuing to operate with Stena Line for at least another 10-15 years. In 2020 she was the oldest ship in the fleet.

Götaverken Arendal Ab, Göteborg, Sweden, 1981
14,378g *(orig.)*, 17,062g *(1982)*, 24,828g *(2002)*
149 x 26.5 m / Twin screw / 20.5 knots
2,100 pass. *(orig.)*, 1,400 *(1982)*, 1,374 *(2002)*
700 cars *(orig.)*, 500 *(1982)*, 456 *(2002)*

STENA EUROPE
FISHGUARD

Prinsessan Birgitta - 1981

Oy Wärtsilä Ltd, Turku, Finland, 1974
8,753g / 152.4 x 20 m / Twin screw / 23 knots / 1,200 pass. / 320 cars
Stena service: 1981-1989

Ordered in 1974 by Sessan Linjen as Prinsessan Birgitta for their
Göteborg–Frederikshavn link, she was acquired by Stena Line in 1981 and
renamed Stena Scandinavica one year later. In 1987 she was chartered to
Cotunav and renamed Scandinavica, then to Sealink British Ferries in 1988.
In 1990, she was sold to Norway Line and renamed the Venus.

Prinsessan Désirée - 1981

Aalborg Værft A/S, Aalborg, Denmark, 1971
5,694g / 123.4 x 19.6 m / Twin screw / 18 knots / 1,400 pass. / 230 cars
Stena service: 1981-1990

Built in 1971 for Sessan Linjen, the Prinsessan Désirée was placed on
the Göteborg–Frederikshavn link. In 1981, Sessan Linjen was acquired by
Stena Line, and the ship was chartered by B&I Line and Sealink. In 1982 she
operated with Sally Line between Ramsgate and Dunkerque as the Viking 2.
In 1983, she was renamed Europafärjan for the Varberg–Grenaa route. In
1987, renamed Lion Princess, she continued on service Kattegat links until
sold in 1993 to Scandi Lines, becoming their Bohus between Strömstad–
Sandefjord, and then later under Color Line until she was sold in 2019.

Prinsessan Christina - 1982

Aalborg Værft A/S, Aalborg, Denmark, 1969
5,679g / 123.4 x 19.6 m / Twin screw / 20.5 knots / 1,400 pass. / 360 cars
Stena service: 1982-1999

Initially ordered by Sessan Linjen as Prinsessan Christina for the Göteborg–
Frederikshavn route, she was renamed Safe Christina in 1981 and chartered
to Sally Line for their Ramsgate–Dunkerque service. In 1982, she was sold
to Stena Line, and renamed again the Prinsessan Christina. In 1983 she was
renamed Stena Nordica, and in 1985 she was
transferred to the Lion Ferry Kattegat routes
as Europafärjan I. Renamed in 1987 as Lion
Prince, then Stena Prince. Sold in 1999 to
Italian interests, renamed Commodore and
later in 2003 as Palau. Resold to C-Beds in
2008 as Wind Solution and further renamed
in 2018 as Aqua Solution.

Prinsessan Birgitta - 1982

Götaverken Arendal Ab, Göteborg, Sweden, 1981
14,368g / 149 x 26 m / Twin screw / 19.5 knots / 2,100 pass. / 700 cars
Stena service: 1982-1983, 1990-1996

*The sistership to the Kronprinsessan Victoria was chartered to Sealink
for the Harwich–Hook of Holland service as the St Nicholas in 1982. Sold
to Rederi AB Gotland in 1989, she remained with Sealink. After the line's
takeover by Stena Line, the St Nicholas was transferred to a new Southampton–Cherbourg service as the Stena Normandy. Chartered to Tallink in 1997
as the Normandy, then to Irish Ferries in 1998, who purchased her in 1999.*

Stena Baltica - 1983

Oy Wärtsilä Ab, Åbo, Finland, 1973
8,528g / 127.8 x 22 m / Twin screw / 19 knots
1,200 pass. / 359 cars / 540 lane metres
Stena service: 1983

*Built as the Bore I for service with Silja Line's between Turku–Mariehamn–
Stockholm. Renamed Skandia in 1980 and after various operations in the
Baltic she was sold to Stena Line in October 1983 and renamed Stena
Baltica. A few days later she was re-sold to USSR Baltic Shipping Co. and
renamed Ilich.*

Stena Jutlandica - 1983

Chantiers du Nord et de la Méditerranée, Dunkerque, France, 1983
16,494g (orig.), 28,559g (1996) / 154.9 x 28.5 m / Twin screw / 20 knots
2,204 pass.(orig.), 1,500 (1996) / 600 cars / 1,640 lane metres
Stena service: 1983-1986, 1990-1997

*Initially placed on the Frederikshavn–Göteborg service, the Stena
Jutlandica was transferred to Dover–Calais in 1996 as the Stena Empereur.
Transferred to P&O Stena Line in 1998 and known as Empereur, then POSL
Provence. Transferred to P&O Ferries in August 2002 and renamed Pride of
Provence. Became the Pride of Telemark in 2004 for service in Scandinavia.
Following a collision in 2007 she had to be later sold for scrap.*

Stena Baltica - 1983

Dubigeon Normandie S.A., Nantes, France, 1971
10,513g / 142.1 x 22.2 m / Twin screw / 20 knots
874 pass. / 250 cars / 420 lane metres
Stena service: 1984

*Built in France as Massalia in 1971, she was one of three similar ferries, the
others being the Eagle of Southern Ferries and Bolero of Fred. Olsen Line.
Sold to Stena in 1984 and renamed Stena Baltica, she was later chartered
to SeaEscape as the Scandinavian Star. In 1990, she operated for DA-NO
Linjen between Oslo–Frederikshavn, but on April 7th a fire broke out on
board claiming 158 lives. She was later rebuilt and renamed Regal Voyager.*

Stena Danica - 1983

Work started on this ship in 1980 at Chantiers du Nord et de la Méditerranée, Dunkirk in France. Due to industrial problems, her delivery was very late and she did not enter service until March 1983 on the Göteborg–Frederikshavn route.

The *Stena Danica* has only operated between Sweden and Denmark since entering service. In 2002 she was chartered for a cruise to the start of the Volvo Ocean Race from her homeport of Göteborg. Later in the year she underwent a major refit with a new restaurant, children's play area and a Stena Plus Lounge being added.

In 2009 further rebuilding works were undertaken to the vessel at Lloyd Werft, in Germany. Today she maintains the Göteborg–Frederikshavn link with the *Stena Jutlandica* and *Stena Vinga*.

Chantiers du Nord & de Méditerranée, Dunkerque, France, 1983
15,899g (orig.), 28,727g (2002)
152.3 x 28 m (orig.), 154.9 x 28 m (2002)
Twin screw / 20 knots / 2,300 pass. / 150 crew
630 cars / 1,640 lane metres

Stena Driver - 1984

Nuovi Cantieri Aquania S.p.A. Marina De Carra, Italy, 1982
13,294g / 171 x 25.3 m / Twin screw / 17.5 knots
548 pass. / 291 cars / 69 lorries / 1,070 lane m.

In 1984 the Greek Lucky Rider was purchased at auction by Stena Line and renamed Stena Driver for the Göteborg–Travemünde link. In 1985 she was sold to Sealink British Ferries and renamed Seafreight Freeway. From 1988 to 2015 she operated in the Baltic under various names and operations. In 2015 she was back under the Stena flag as the Stena Gothica.

Stena Nordica - 1986

Ateliers & Chantiers du Havre, France, 1973
6,801g / 128.1 x 20 m / Twin screw / 19 knots
1,500 pass. / 270 cars
Stena service: 1986-1988

Built as the Peter Wessel for Larvik Line for their service between Larvik–Frederikshavn and out of season charter work. In late 1985 sold to Stena AB and renamed the Stena Nordica. The following year put on the Moss–Frederikshavn–Göteborg link. In 1988 sold to Jadrolinija and renamed Marko Polo. Still in service.

Stena Germanica - 1987

The *Stena Germanica* was the first of four large ferries ordered in 1980 by Stena Line for Scandinavian routes. She was launched in August 1981 as *the Stena Scandinavica*.

However, due to problems at the construction yard in Poland, completion was delayed, and it was not until 1987 that she entered service as the *Stena Germanica* on the overnight

Kiel–Göteborg route, joined in 1988 by the second of the quartet, the *Stena Scandinavica.*

In 2010 in the light of increased competition from air travel, decline in the traditional mini-cruise market and a demand for more freight space, the *Stena Germanica* was replaced by *Stena Hollandica* from the Harwich–Hoek van Holland route.

Following a major rebuilding programme, she was renamed the *Stena Vision* for new role between Sweden and Poland. In her original layout, the *Stena Germanica* had berths for 2,374 passengers and space for 550 cars, following her refit her accommodation was reduced to 1,700 passengers. Her vehicle decks can now take 550 cars/120 trailers for her role on the Karlskrona–Gdynia route.

Gdynia Stocznia i Komuni Paryski, Poland, 1987
24,967g (orig.), 26,071g (1988), 39,178g (1999)
175.4 x 29 m (orig.), 175.4 x 30.8 m (1988)
Twin screw / 20.5 knots / 2,374 pass. / 145 crew
700 cars / 90 lorries / 1,628 lane metres

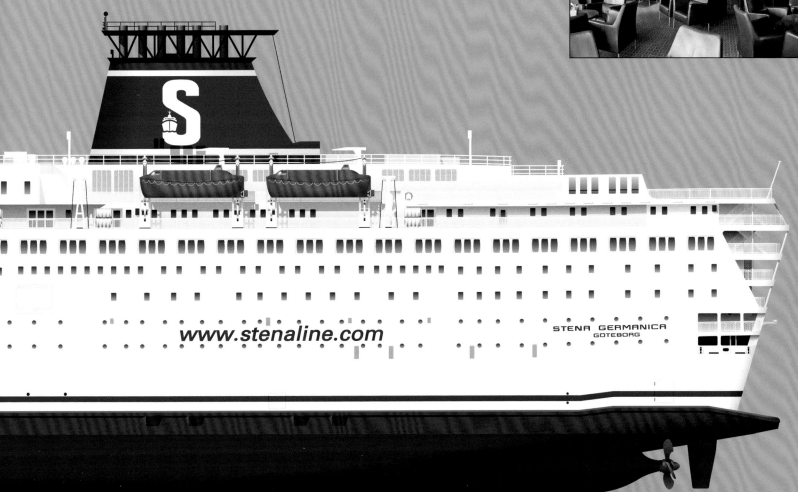

www.stenaline.com

STENA GERMANICA
GÖTEBORG

Princess Marguerite - 1988

Fairfield Shipsbuilders & Engineers Co Ltd, Govan, Scotland 1949
5,911g / 113.9 x 17.1 m / Twin screw / 23 knots / 1,800 pass. / 50 cars
Stena service: 1988-1991

The Princess Marguerite was constructed in Scotland in 1949 for Canadian Pacific's British Columbia Coast Steamships. In 1988 BCCS was sold for $6 million to the B.C. Stena Line, a subsidiary of the Swedish ferry operator. But the Swedish involvement in Canada was short-lived, and in 1992 the Princess Marguerite was sold in Asia and converted into a Singapore-based gambling ship. She was finally scrapped at Alang, India in 1997.

Stena Scandinavica - 1988

Stocznia im Lenina, Gdansk, Poland, 1988
26,088g (orig.), 39,178g (1999) / 175.4 x 29 m (orig.), 175.4 x 31 m (1999)
Twin screw / 21.5 knots / 2,500 pass. / 145 crew
700 cars / 90 lorries / 1,628 lane metres

Sister to the Stena Germanica, she was launched 1983 in Poland. Completed at a Swedish shipyard due to industrial problems at Gdansk shipyard. Eventually delivered on February 1988 to Stena Line. Baptized by Godmother HM Queen Silvia in Kiel in Germany. In 2011, she was withdrawn from the Göteborg–Kiel service and rebuilt for her new role on the Karlskrona–Gdynia route, like her sister. She was renamed Stena Spirit.

Vancouver Island Princess - 1988

A. Stephen & Sons Ltd, Glasgow, Scotland, 1955
5,554g / 126.8 x 20 m / Twin screw / 17 knots / 1,000 pass. / 130 cars
Stena service: 1988-1993

Delivered in 1955 as the Princess Of Vancouver to Canadian Pacific Railway Co. for their Vancouver–Naaimo route, she was renamed Vancouver Island Princess in 1985 for the Comex–Powell River service and then later Seattle–Victoria. In 1988 she was sold to British Columbia Stena Line Co, which was closed down after only two years. After various charters she was sold to the Government of China renamed the Nan Hai Ming Zhu.

Stena Arcadia - 1988

Kynossoura Dock Yard Ltd, Kynossoura, Salamis, Greece, 1974
8,500g (orig.), 7,764g (1991) / 132 x 19.8 m / Twin screw / 18 knots
1,600 pass. / 250 cars
Stena service: 1988-1994

Delivered in May 1974 to Hellenic Mediterranean Lines as the Castalia for service between Brindisi and Patras. After her sale in 1988 and various charter work, she became the Stena Arcadia in 1994 for service in Italy. Three years later she was sold to Empress Cruise of the Bahamas and renamed the Emerald Empress.

Stena Baltica - 1988

Werft Nobiskrug GmbH, Rendsburg, Germany, 1973
5,829g / 118.7 x 18.3 m / Twin screw / 22.5 knots
1,100 pass. / 225 cars / 444 lane metres
Stena service: 1988-1989

Built as the Prinz Hamlet *for Prinzen Line, for service between Hamburg - Harwich. In 1987 she was purchased by DFDS, but after only a year in service she was sold to Stena RoRo and renamed* Stena Baltica. *Never used for traffic with Stena Line. Chartered and later sold to Polish Zegluga Baltyska, Kolobrzeg, Poland and renamed* Nieborow.

Stena Nordica - 1988

Oy Wärtsilä Ab, Åbo, Finland, 1979
10,604g / 136.1 x 24.2 m / Twin screw / 21.5 knots / 1,800 pass. / 425 cars
Stena service: 1988-1997

Built as the Turella *in 1979 for Viking Line consortium member SF Line and used on the Kapellskär–Mariehamn–Naantali route. Sold in 1988 to Stena Line. Renamed* Stena Nordica *and placed on Göteborg–Frederikshavn service. Transferred to their Lion Ferry subsidiary in 1996 as the* Lion King. *Purchased by Tallink in 1997 and renamed* Fantaasia *for use on their Stockholm to Tallinn route. She lives on today as Ventouris' Ferries* Rigel III.

Silvia Regina - 1988

Oy Wärtsilä Ab Perno / Turku, Finland, 1981
25,905g (orig.), 33,967g (2000) / 166.1 x 29 m / Twin screw / 22 knots
2,000 pass. / 450 cars / 70 lorries

Ordered by Rederi Ab Svea and entered service on the Stockholm–Helsinki link in 1981. Sold to Stena Line in 1988, she continued to operate in the Baltic until 1991, when she was renamed Stena Britannica *for the Harwich–Hoek van Holland route. Renamed* Stena Saga *in 1994 and transferred to the Oslo–Fredrikshavn service. In March 2020 she was withdrawn from service and put up for sale as part of a reduction of operations due to Covid-19.*

Koningin Beatrix - 1989

Van der Giessen De Noord, Krimpen an de Ijssel, Holland, 1986
31,189g (orig.), 31,910g (2005) / 161.8 x 24.6 m (orig.), 164.6 x 27.6 m (2005)
Twin screw / 20 knots / 2,000 pass. / 500 cars / 1,800 lane metres
Stena service: 1989-2013

The 1986-built Koningin Beatrix *was used on SMZ's joint Harwich–Hoek van Holland service with Sealink. In 1989, the SMZ (Crown Line) operation was sold to Stena Line BV. The ship was transferred in 1997 to the Fishguard–Rosslare route, then in 2002 to the Karlskrona–Gdynia route and renamed* Stena Baltica. *In 2013 sold to SNAV in Italy and renamed* SNAV Adriatico.

Stena Seatrader - 1989

A/S Nakskov Skibsværft, Nakskov, Denmark, 1973
17,991g / 182.7 x 22.1 m / Twin screw / 17.5 knots
236 pass. / 2,100 lane metres
Stena service: 1989-2008

Built as the Finncarrier for Finnlines service between Helsinki, Lübeck and Copenhagen. For the next 20 years she operated various services in the Baltic. Purchased by Stena Line in 1990 and renamed Stena Seatrader. She was chartered out for various operations in the USA, Irish Sea and in 1995 after a major overhaul she was placed on the Göteborg - Kiel service, then later on the Harwich/ Killingholme-Hoek van Holland link. Sold in 2008.

Stena Antrim - 1990

Harland & Wolff Ltd, Belfast, Northern Ireland, 1981
7,399g / 129.6 x 21.6 m / Twin screw / 19.5 knots
1,170 pass. / 309 cars / 744 lane metres
Stena service: 1990-1998

Built as the St Christopher for the Sealink operations between Dover and Calais. She was re-built in 1983 to offer improved passenger areas including a large supermarket. In 1990 she was sold to Stena Line, operating on the Irish Sea and between Newhaven and Dieppe as the Stena Antrim. Sold to Lignes Maritimes du Detroit SA, Casablanca, Morocco in 1998 and renamed Ibn Batouta for service between Tangier and Algeciras.

Cambridge Ferry - 1990

Hawthorne, Leslie Shipbuilders Ltd, Hebburn, England, 1963
3,061g / 122.8 x 18.7 m / Twin screw / 13.5 knots
100 pass. / 35 railway wagons or 250 cars
Stena service: 1990-1992

Built for the British Transport Commission for the train ferry service between Harwich and Zeebrugge. In 1990 sold to Stena Line AB for freight services from Fishguard to Rosslare and for refit periods at Holyhead and Stranraer. In 1992 sold to Sincomar, Valletta, Malta and renamed Ita Uno.

Stena Caledonia - 1990

Harland & Wolff Ltd, Belfast, Northern Ireland, 1981
7,197g (orig.), 12,619g (2000) / 129.6 x 21 m (orig.), 132 x 21.6 m (2000)
Twin screw / 19.5 knots / 1,154 pass. / 309 cars / 744 lane metres
Stena service: 1990-2011

Built as the St David for service between Holyhead and Dun Laoghaire, initially as back up vessel to the St Columba in busy periods and for other relief work in the fleet. Spent most of her time on Stranraer–Larne services. Acquired by Stena Line in 1990 and renamed Stena Caledonia. Sold in 2012..

Stena Felicity - 1990

Öresundsvarvet Ab, Landskrona, Sweden, 1980
14,932g / 142.6 x 24.5 m / Twin screw / 21 knots / 2,072 pass. / 515 cars
Stena Line service: 1990-1997

Built as the Visby in 1980 for Rederi AB Gotland. In 1990 she was chartered to Sealink for their Fishguard–Rosslare service and renamed Felicity. Later renamed Stena Felicity. In 1997 she was returned to Rederi AB Gotland, and re-entered Gotland service in 1998 under her original name Visby. In 2003 she was sold to Polska Zegluga Baltyska and renamed Scandinavia for Polferries' Gdansk–Nynäshamn service.

Stena Fantasia - 1990

Av Kockums Varv Ab, Malmö, Sweden, 1980
25,122g / 163.5 x 27.6 m / Twin screw / 21.5 knots / 1,800 pass. / 500 cars
Stena service: 1990-1998

Built as the Scandinavia in 1980 and later sold to Bulgarian interests and renamed Tzarevetz. The ship then operated for various companies until she was purchased by Sealink and renamed Fiesta prior to a major conversion. Entered service on Dover–Calais route as the Fantasia, then Stena Fantasia after Sealink's takeover by Stena. In 1998 she was renamed P&OSL Canterbury under P&O Stena Line. Sold to GA Ferries in 2004.

Stena Cambria - 1990

Harland & Wolff Ltd, Belfast, Northern Ireland, 1980
7,405g / 129.4 x 21 m / Twin screw / 19.5 knots
1,400 pass. / 309 cars / 744 lane metres
Stena service: 1990-1999

Built as the St Anselm for the Flagship Dover-Calais service. Spent most of her time on the English Channel until 1990 when she was renamed Stena Cambria and placed on the Irish Sea operations of Stena Line. Final period of operations in British waters in 1999 on the Newhaven–Dieppe route operating for P&O Stena Line. Sold to Spain and renamed Isla de Botafoc.

Stena Galloway - 1990

Harland & Wolff Ltd, Belfast, Northern Ireland, 1980
6,630g / 129.4 x 21.6 m / Twin screw / 18.5 knots
974 pass. / 309 cars / 744 lane metres
Stena service: 1990-2002

Built in 1980 as the Galloway Princess for service between Stranraer and Larne. Sold to Stena Line with the rest of the Sealink fleet, she was renamed Stena Galloway in 1991. Sold in 2002 to International Maritime Transport Corporation (IMTC) of Casablanca, Morocco, and renamed Le Rif for services between Tangier and Algeciras.

Stena Hengist - 1990

Arsenal de la Marine Nationale Française, Brest, France, 1972
5,596g / 118.1 x 19.8 m / Twin screw / 19.5 knots / 1,400 pass. / 256 cars
Stena service: 1990-1992

Built as the Hengist in 1972 for Folkestone to Calais/Boulogne services and overnight sailings from Folkestone to Oostende. Her sisters were Horsa and Senlac. In 1990 she passed to the ownership of Stena Line and became the Stena Hengist. Sold in 1992 to GA Ferries as Romilda, passing to Ventouris Sea Lines the following year as Apollo Express 2. Scrapped in 2017.

Stena Hibernia - 1990

Aalborg Værft A/S, Aalborg, Denmark, 1977
7,836g / 129.2 x 21.2 m / Twin screw / 19.5 knots / 1,700 pass. / 336 cars
Stena service: 1990-1997

Built as the St Columba for the Holyhead–Dun Laoghaire link. She was only to operate on this link apart from a short period in 1982 when she covered the Fishguard operations. In 1991 she was renamed Stena Hibernia after a major overhaul at Lloyd Werft in Bremerhaven. Following the introduction of the HSS service in 1996, she was downgraded as reserve vessel as the Stena Adventurer. Sold in 1997 to Greece and renamed Express Aphrodite.

Stena Horsa - 1990

When in 1984, the Sealink ownership passed to Sea Containers, the 1972-built *Horsa* and her sister the *Hengist* continued to run for Sealink British Ferries from Folkestone to Calais and Boulogne. The new owners made a major investment in both the *Hengist* and *Horsa* at Folkestone in 1986 to allow them to tie in with Sea Containers' Orient Express operations, which saved the service from closure in the years before 1990.

The *Horsa* was replaced by the *St Anselm* on the Folkestone services in 1990 and was moved away from the Dover Strait for the first time onto the Holyhead–Dun Laoghaire summer services. The following year the *St Anselm* (now *Stena Cambria*) exchanged places with the now renamed *Stena Horsa*. The sisters were re-united for one final season on the Folkestone

route. Stena Line were keen to both save money after the purchase of Sealink from Sea Containers and also focus traffic on the Dover–Calais service. Folkestone lost its Boulogne link after 148 years on 31 December 1991, when the *Stena Horsa* made the final crossing.

In 1992, *Stena Horsa* was sold to Agoudimos Lines for a service linking Rafina, Andros, Tinos and Mykonos as the *Penelope A*.

Arsenal de la Marine Nationale Française, Brest, France, 1972
5,590g / 118.1 x 19.8 m / Twin screw / 19.5 knots
1,400 pass. / 256 cars
Stena service: 1990–1992

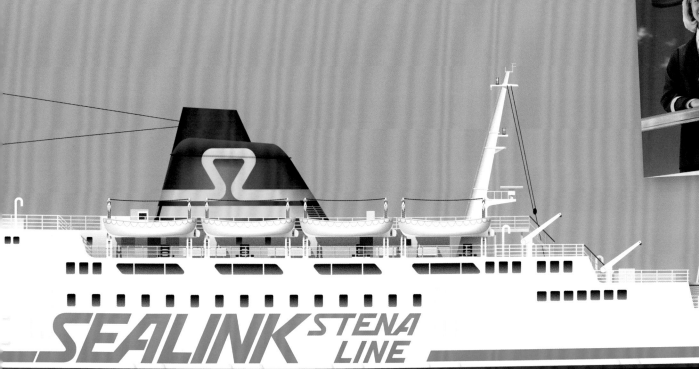

Stena Challenger - 1991

Completed in 1991 for the Stena Group's chartering division Stena RoRo, the *Stena Challenger* was named in honour of the lost space shuttle, one of the Stena companies having been involved in salvaging the remains of the exploded spacecraft. The new ship's hull was constructed in Sweden before being towed to Norway for completion and, upon delivery, she was immediately transferred to Stena's newly acquired Sealink

STENA CHALLENGER

SEALINK STE LI

subsidiary and placed on Dover–Calais/Dunkirk links, entering service in June 1991. With her extended accommodation she could carry 500 passengers. Her near sister was the *Stena Traveller*.

In September 1995 she ran aground off Calais in severe weather. Eventually she was towed away to Dunkirk for inspection and repairs. In September 1996 she was transferred to the Irish Sea to run on the new Holyhead–Dublin service.

In April 2000 she was sold to Marine Atlantic, Canada, and placed on their North Sydney–Port Aux Basques/Argentia route as *Leif Ericson*.

Bruce Verkstad Ab, Landskrona / Fosen Mekaniske Verksted, Feevag, Norway, 1991
18,523g / 157.3 x 24.3 m / Twin screw / 19.5 knots
500 pass. / 480 cars / 1,800 lane metres
Stena service: 1991-2001

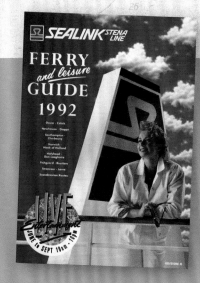

STENA CHALLENGER
DOVER

Stena Invicta - 1991

Nakskov Skibsværft, Nakskov, Denmark, 1985
19,763g / 137 x 24.6 m / Twin screw / 17.5 knots / 1,720 pass. / 370 cars
Stena service: 1991-2000

Built as the Peder Paars for the Århus–Kalundborg route. Sold in 1990 to Stena Line AB for delivery in May 1991. Renamed Stena Invicta and chartered to Sealink Stena Line for the Dover–Calais route. After a short period of service on the Irish Sea in 1999, she was chartered to Color Line one year later and put on their Strömstad–Sandefjord as the Color Viking. Sold in 2001 to Color Line for NOK 145 million.

Stena Nautica - 1991

Nakskov Skibsværft, Nakskov, Denmark, 1986
19,504g / 135.5 x 24.6 m / Twin screw / 17.5 knots / 1,720 pass. / 370 cars

Built as the Niels Klim for the Århus–Kalundborg route and sister to the Stena Invicta. Sold to Stena Line in 1990 and renamed Stena Nautica. Chartered out to Irish Ferries in 1992 and renamed the Isle of Innisfree (Rosslare–Pembroke Dock route). Became the Lion King in 1995 for Stena Line's subsidiary company Lion Ferry. Renamed Stena Nautica in 1996, then chartered out for three years before returning to Stena Line operations on the Kattegat.

Auersberg - 1992 (chartered)

VEB Mathias Thesen Werft, Wismar, East Germany, 1983
4,961g / 138.1 x 20.5 m / Twin screw / 14.5 knots
12 pass. / 1,089 lane m.
Stena Line service: 1992

Delivered in June 1983 to VEB Deutfracht/Seereederei GmbH, Rostock, East Germany. Deployed on various shipping routes until 1992 when she was chartered to Sealink Stena Line for the Holyhead–Dun Laoghaire to cover for refits. Later to service in the Baltic, Spain and Greece. Sold for scrap in 2010.

Stena Traveller - 1992

Bruce Verkstad Ab, Landskrona / Fosen Mekaniske Verksted, Rissa, Norway, 1991
18,332g / 154 x 24.3 m / Twin screw / 18 knots
204 pass. / 480 cars / 1,800 lane metres
Stena service: 1992, 1995-1997, 2002-2004

A near sister to the Stena Challenger, she briefly operated on the Harwich–Hoek van Holland and Southampton–Cherbourg routes prior to a 3-year charter to TT Line as the TT Traveller which would repeat between 1997 and 2002. Sold to DFDS in 2004 and renamed Lisco Patria, then Patria Seaways.

Stena Sea Lynx II - 1994 (chartered)

InCat, Hobart, Tasmania, Australia, 1994
3,898g / 77.5 x 26 m / Quadr. waterjet / 37 knots / 612 pass. / 135 cars
Stena service: 1994-1996, 1996-1998

Launched as InCat 033 and then chartered out to Stena Line AB, Göteborg and renamed the Stena Sea Lynx II for the Holyhead–Dun Laoghaire route. In 1996 renamed Stena Lynx II. Placed on the Dover–Calais route in 1996, she operated between Newhaven and Dieppe the following year to the end of her charter with Stena Line in 1998.

Stena Sea Lynx - 1993 (chartered)

InCat, Hobart, Tasmania, Australia, 1993
3,331g / 73.6 x 26 m / Quadr. waterjet / 35 knots / 582 pass. / 88 cars
Stena service: 1993-1996, 1996-1998

Delivered in June 1993 to Buquebus and then chartered to Stena Sealink Line for their new fast ferry service between Holyhead–Dun Laoghaire, then Fishguard–Rosslare the following year. Renamed Stena Lynx for service at Holyhead and later transferred to the Newhaven–Dieppe route. She later operated at Dover in 1997 before she was handed back to her owners in 1998.

Condor 10 - 1996 (chartered)

InCat, Hobart, Tasmania, Australia, 1992
3,241g / 74.3 x 26 m / Quadr. waterjet / 39 knots
580 pass. / 90 cars
Stena service: 1996

Ordered by Condor Ferries in 1991 for their Weymouth–Guernsey–Jersey service. Entered service in April 1993. The craft undertook various charter work in New Zealand and Finland before being chartered by Stena Line for their Fishguard–Rosslare link in 1996.

Stena Explorer - 1996

HSS 1500 was the name of a model of Stena HSS craft developed and operated by Stena Line on their European international ferry routes, a semi-small-waterplane-area twin hull (SWATH) catamaran designed with the aim of providing a comfortable and fast service in most weather conditions. Powered by

four GE Aviation gas turbines, the *Stena Explorer* and her two sisters were the largest high-speed craft ever built in the world.

The HSS were designed to allow quick turnarounds at each port, in 30 minutes or less. A specially designed linkspan had to be built at each port for them, providing ropeless mooring and also allowing for quick loading, unloading and servicing. Vehicles were loaded via two of the four stern doors and parked in a 'U' configuration.

The accommodation for passengers was on an open plan design and included

a number of modern food franchise outlets. Three vessels were ultimately completed between 1996 and 1997. The first of the class, *Stena Explorer* entered service in April 1996 on the Holyhead–Dun Laoghaire route. The continued escalation in oil prices was eventually to see the demise of these series of craft. The *Stena Explorer* was withdrawn in 2014.

Finnyards, Rauma, Finland, 1996
19,638g / 126.6 x 40 m / Quadr. waterjet / 40 knots
1,500 pass. / 375 cars
Stena service: 1996-2015

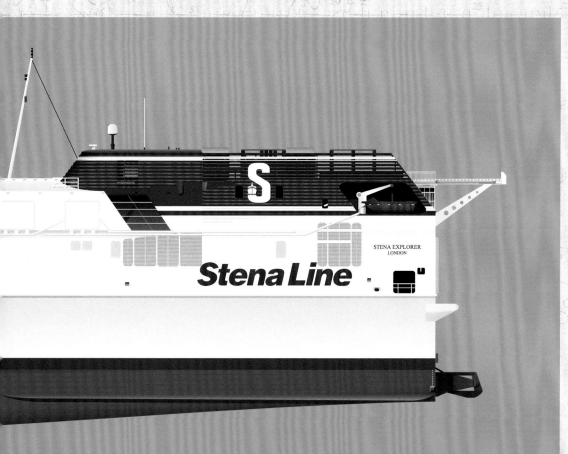

InCat, Hobart, Tasmania, Australia, 1996
4,113g / 80.6 x 26 m / Quadr. waterjet / 37 knots
670 pass. / 148 cars
Stena service: 1996-2011

Delivered in May to American Fast Ferries Ltd and then chartered to Stena for their Dover–Calais route in 1996. Renamed Elite for the joint P&O Stena Line service from Newhaven to Dieppe. Later renamed P&OSL Elite and in 2004 returned to her original name Stena Lynx III for the Fishguard–Rosslare service. Until 2011 she remained on the Irish Sea with Stena Line before she was sold to Korean interests.

Fincantieri S.p.A., Riva Trigoso, Italy, 1996
3,750g / 95 x 16 m / Quadr. waterjet / 36 knots
580 pass. / 173 cars
Stena service: 1996-1997

Operated by Stena Line AB on a short-term charter in 1996 and renamed Stena Pegasus for service between Newhaven and Dieppe. Returned to her owners at the end of the year becoming the Pegasus One again. Later sold to Venezuela.

Stena Jutlandica - 1996

The *Stena Jutlandica* was built for the Göteborg–Frederikshavn route as a Ro-Pax ship and also a train ferry. She was the first of a series of similar ships built by Van der Giessen de Noord. The second vessel was the *Isle of Inishmore*, followed by the *Mont St Michel*. A smaller series ships, the *Ben-my-Chree* and *Commodore Clipper* where also modelled around the hull design of the *Stena Jutlandica*.

Launched in March 1996 as the *Stena Jutlandica,* the vessel was briefly renamed *Stena Jutlandica III* prior to entering service. In August 1996 she returned to her original name following

the transfer of the previous *Stena Jutlandica* to the English Channel.

In March 2018 Stena Line announced the plan to convert the ship to electric propulsion with a 1 MWh battery pack. So far, the 'Jutlandica' has only operated on the Göteborg and Frederikshavn route.

Van der Giessen De Noord, Krimpen an de Ijssel, Holland, 1996
29,691g / 182.3 x 28.4 m / Twin screw / 21.5 knots / 1,500 pass. / 550 cars / 600 lane metres

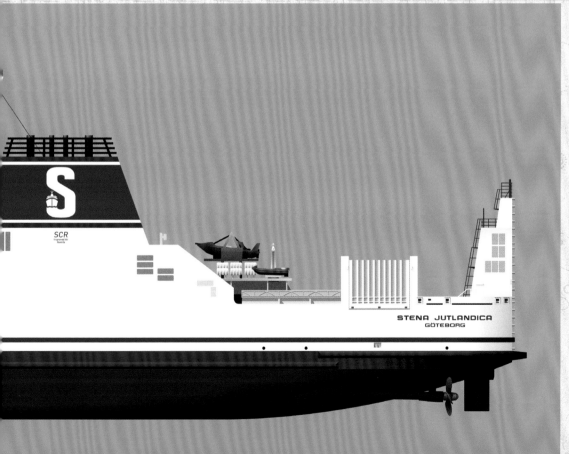

Stena Voyager - 1996

Finnyards, Rauma, Finland, 1996
19,638g / 126.6 x 40 m / Quadr. waterjet / 40 knots
1,500 pass. / 375 cars
Stena service: 1996-2013

Delivered in June 1996 to Stena Line and opened the new HSS service in July between Stranraer and Belfast. In 1998 she saw service on the Hoek van Holland–Harwich link during the refit of her near sister. In November 2011 she completed her last sailings in the light of new tonnage on the North Channel. Two years later she was broken up after only twelve years in service.

Stena Carisma - 1997

Westamarin A/S, Kristiansand / West Bygg A/S, Norway, 1997
8,631g / 88 x 30 m / Twin waterjet / 40 knots
900 pass. / 210 cars

Built in 1997 and designed on a smaller scale to that of the HSS 1500 craft (HSS 900). Entered service on the Göteborg–Frederikshavn link in June 1997. The vessel proved very expensive to operate and eventually had to be withdrawn. Currently laid up at Göteborg since 2013.

Stena Royal - 1998

N.V. Boelwerf S.A, Temse, Belgium, 1991
28,883g / 163.4 x 27.7 m / Twin screw / 21.5 knots
1,400 pass. / 710 cars / 1,745 lane metres
Stena service: 1998-1999

Built in 1991 for RMT as the Prins Filip for their Ostend–Dover link, which eventually closed in 1997. In 1998 Stena Line acquired the vessel for charter work and renamed her the Stena Royal. She was to operate on six different English Channel services over the next twelve years until DFDS purchased her for their Dover–Calais route in 2012 and renamed her Calais Seaways.

Stena Discovery - 1997

Finnyards, Rauma, Finland, 1997
19,638g / 126.6 x 40 m / Quadr. waterjet / 40 knots
1,500 pass. / 375 cars
Stena service: 1997-2009

Arrived at Hoek van Holland for the first time May 1997. For just under ten years the Stena Discovery operated the route before she was withdrawn in favour once again of a conventional ferry operation. Her internal accommodation was different to that of her sisters, reflecting the longer service route. Eventually sold to Venezuelan interests in 2009.

Aurora Af Helsingborg - 1999

Tangen Verft A/S, Kragerö, Norway, 1992
10,918g / 111.2 x 28.2 m / Twin pods (2 sets) / 14 knots
1,250 pass. / 240 cars / 535 lane metres
Stena service: 1999-2008

Ordered for SweFerry Ab (Scandlines) for operations between Helsingborg and Helsingör. In November 1999 she was sold by SweFerry AB to Stena AB. In 2008, the ship was sold back to Scandlines AB, Helsingborg. Continues in service in 2020.

Skåne - 1999

Astilleros Españoles, Puerta Real, Spain, 1998
42,705g / 199 x 29.6 m / Twin screw / 21 knots
600 pass. / 500 cars / 3,295 lane metres

The Skåne is the world's largest multi-purpose RoRo/Train ferry. She is now owned by Stena Line and was built by Astilleros Españoles (AESA) in Puerto Real in Spain. She was delivered in June 1998 and operates between Trelleborg in Sweden and Rostock in Germany.

Trelleborg - 2000

Öresundsvarvet Ab, Landskrona, Sweden, 1981
20,028g / 170.2 x 23.8 m / Twin screw / 19 knots
800 pass. / 680 lane metres
Stena service: 1999-2016

Built for the Trelleborg–Sassnitz operation. In 1999 transferred to the ownership of Stena Line. In 2016 sold to MH Marine Co, Majuro, Marshall Island and renamed Salam 2.

Götaland - 2000

A/S Nakskov Skibsværft, Nakskov, Denmark, 1973
18,060g / 182 x 22.5 m / Twin screw / 18.5 knots
400 pass. / 753 lane metres
Stena service: 1999-2010

Built for the Trelleborg–Sassnitz service. In 1992 she was rebuilt with her superstructure raised by 2.7 metres. Further extension work was carried out in 1993. Brought into Stena Line fleet in 1999, the Götaland was sold in 2010 to Russian interests and renamed Apollonia.

Stena Britannica - 2000

Astilleros Españoles, Puerta Real, Spain, 2000
33,769g / 188.1 x 28.7 m / Twin screw / 22 knots
440 pass. / 300 cars (2010) / 2,918 lane metres
Stena service: 2000-2003

Delivered on 25 August 2000 to Stena Line for the Harwich-Hoek van Holland service. After three years on the link she was sold to Finnlines and renamed Finnfellow, for operations on their Helsinki–Travemünde route.

Stena Hollandica - 2001

Built as the *Stena Hollandica* by Astilleros Españoles shipyard in Puerto Real, Spain, the *Stena Hollandica* was the last of four 'Seapacer' class ships built by this yard for Stena Line: the *Finnclipper* and *Finneagle* in 1998 (chartered to Finnish ferry operator Finnlines) and the *Stena Britannica* and *Stena Hollandica* in 2000.

The *Stena Hollandica* entered service between Harwich and Hoek van Holland on 9th March 2001. In January 2007, the high-speed ferry *Stena Discovery* was withdrawn from service and to accommodate the extra traffic the *Stena Hollandica* was sent to the Lloyd Werft yard in Bremerhaven in March 2007 for lengthening. The vessel was cut in two

The *Stena Hollandica* before lengthening.

vertically and a 52-metre section was inserted, making it one of the biggest jumboisation programmes ever made to a RoPax vessel.

In May 2010, *Stena Hollandica* was replaced on the Harwich–Hook Van Holland route by the first of two 62,000 ton superferries. The former *Stena*

Hollandica was sent for an extensive refit at the Remontowa shipyard in Gdansk, prior to re-entering service in August 2010 on the Göteborg–Kiel route as the *Stena Germanica III*. She was renamed *Stena Germanica* a month later.

The *Stena Germanica* is the first vessel in the Stena Line fleet to run on recycled methanol after her conversion in 2015 in Poland.

Astilleros Españoles, Puerta Real, Spain, 2001
29,841g (orig.), 44,237g (2007)
188.3 x 28.7 m (orig.), 240.1 x 28.7 m (2007)
Twin screw / 22 knots /440 pass. (orig.),
900 pass. (2007), 1,200 pass. / 300 cars (2010)
2,500 lane m. (orig.), 4,000 lane m. (2007)

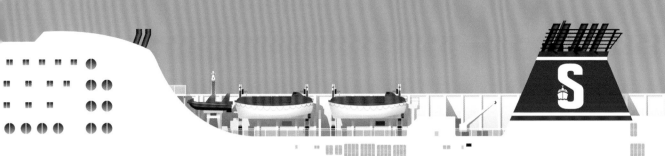

Stena Forwarder - 2001 (chartered)

Cantiere Navale Visentini Francesco & C., Donada, Italy, 2001
25,000g / 186.5 x 25.6 m / Twin screw / 22.5 knots
1,000 pass. / 75 cars / 2,100 lane metres
Stena service: 2001-2003

Delivered to Stena Line on charter for two years in April 2001 for the Dublin–Holyhead freight route. Chartered then to Baja Ferries Lines, Mexico and renamed California Star. Remains in service in 2020 as the Af Claudia.

Stena Britannica - 2003

Hyundai Heavy Industries, Ulsan, South Korea, 2003
43,487g (orig.), 55,050g (2007), 57,639g (2010)
211.6 x 29.9 m (orig.), 241.1 x 29.9 m (2007), 243.3 x 29.9 m (2010)
Twin screw / 22.5 knots / 900 pass. (orig.), 1,300 pass. (2007)
3,400 lane metres (orig.), 4,220 lane metres (2007)

Entered service on the Harwich–Hoek van Holland service in 2003 and remained on the link until October 2010 when she was replaced by larger tonnage. The Stena Britannica was extensively overhauled prior to her transfer to the Gothenburg–Kiel service in 2011 and renamed Stena Scandinavica.

Stena Adventurer - 2003

Hyundai Heavy Industries, Ulsan, South Korea, 2003
43,532g / 211.6 x 29.3 m / Twin screw / 22.5 knots
1,500 pass. / 3,517 lane metres

This sister to the Stena Britannica was built for the Holyhead–Dublin service. Entered operations on the Irish Sea in July 2003. She has only operated on this route since her introduction. In 2019 she was joined by the Stena Estrid as operating partner on this important Central Corridor link between the UK and Ireland.

Stena Nordica - 2004

Mitsubishi Heavy Industries, Shimonoseki, Japan, 2000
24,206g / 170.5 x 25.8 m / Twin screw / 25.7 knots
405 pass. / 375 cars / 1,949 lane metres

Built for P&O as the European Ambassador for their Irish Sea operations. Sold to Stena Line in April 2004 and renamed Stena Nordica. Since her new role with Stena Line she has operated as relief vessel in the Baltic, North Sea and Irish Sea, including being chartered to DFDS for their Dover–Calais service in 2015.

Stena Trader - 2006

Baltijsky Zavod Shipyard, Russia, 2005 / Fosen, Rissa, Norway, 2006
26,002g (orig.), 28,460g (2010) / 212 x 26.7 m (orig.), 200 x 26.7 m (2010)
Twin screw / 22.2 knots / 300 pass. (orig.), 1,000 pass. (2010)
3,100 lane metres (orig.), 2,860 lane metres (2010)
Stena Line service: 2006-2015

Largely built in Russia, her assembly was finished in Norway. Operated by
Stena Line from 2007 to 2010 on the Hoek Van Holland–Killingholme route.
Chartered to Marine Atlantic and entered regular passenger service as Blue
Puttees in early March 2011. In May 2015, Marine Atlantic purchased both
the Stena Trader and her sister Stena Traveller for C$200 million.

Stena Traveller - 2007

Baltijsky Zavod Shipyard, Russia, 2006 / Fosen, Rissa, Norway, 2007
25,900g (orig.), 28,460g (2010) / 212 x 26.7 m (orig.), 200 x 26.7 m (2010)
Twin screw / 22.2 knots / 300 pass. (orig.), 1,000 pass. (2010)
3,100 lane metres (orig.), 2,860 lane metres (2010)
Stena Line service: 2007-2015

Sister to the Stena Trader. Operated on the UK/Dutch services of Stena Line
until December 2010. Sent to Lloyds Werft, Bremerhaven for rebuilding like
her sister following her charter to Canada. Joined her sister on the North
Sydney service in April 2011 as the Highlanders.

Finnarrow - 2007 (chartered)

Pt Dok Kodja Bahri, Jakarta, Indonesia, 1996
29,100g / 168.1 x 28.3 m / 572 pass. / 800 cars
Stena Line service: 2007-2011, 2013

Built as the Gotland for Rederi Ab Gotland for charter work. In 1997 sold
to Finnlines and renamed Finnarrow. In 2013 chartered to Stena Line as
relief ship between Holyhead and Dublin. She was only in service for a short
period following an accident whilst docking at Holyhead.

Stena Navigator - 2009

Dubigeon Normandie S.A., Nantes, France, 1984
15,093g / 130 x 23 m / Twin screw / 18.5 knots
1,800 pass. / 330 cars / 850 lane metres
Stena service: 1992-1997 (chartered), 2009-2012

Built as the Champs-Elysées for SNCF. In 1992 she was chartered to
Stena Line for the Newhaven–Dieppe route and renamed Stena Parisien.
She was returned to SeaFrance (SNCF) in 1997 and renamed SeaFrance
Manet. In 2009 she was sold to Stena Line for the Stranraer–Belfast link
and renamed Stena Navigator. In 2011 she was purchased by Balearia,
becoming the Daniya, then the Poeta López Anglada.

Stena Hollandica - 2010

The *Stena Hollandica* was launched in January 2010, as the first of two identical RoPax ferries built in Germany by Wadan Yards for Stena Line. The total value of the order amounted to approximately €400 million.

Delays arose when Stena temporarily withdrew the order in response to economic difficulties being experienced by Waden Yards. After further negotiations the order was reinstated, but the new agreement included a price cut of 6% or approximately €24 million. Her naming ceremonies took place on 8 June 2010 at the Hoek van Holland.

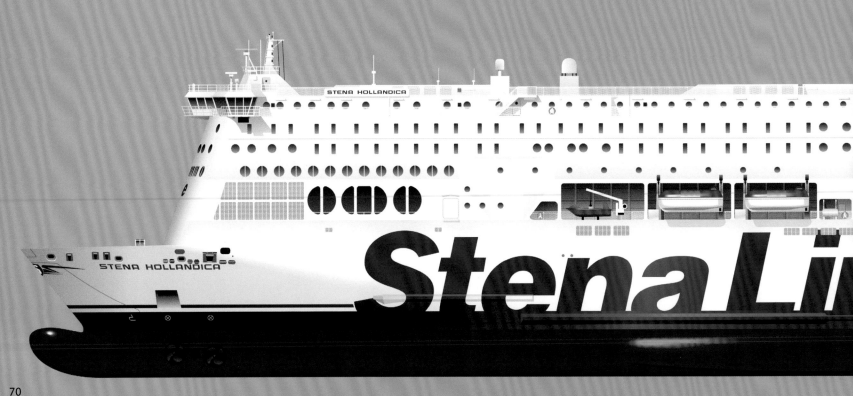

Usually at night the *Stena Hollandica* sails to the Netherlands from Harwich to Hoek van Holland and at daytime she sails back to England. Both ships have proved very popular on the route for both passengers but also with freight operators.

Both ferries were built in accordance with Stena Line's energy savings programme. The hull design was optimised using an advanced coating system. Catalytic converters and engines with better combustion rates help to lower the vessel's environmental impact.

The two sisters' interior, including the public and crew areas, were designed by Swedish company Figura. The company created the general layout, colour schemes and elevations of the bulkheads.

Both ferries have facilities to recycle cardboard, glass and food waste. To reduce the energy used by the ship's cooling system, all windows are superimposed with solar film that blocks 82% of the sun's radiant heat.

Wadan Yards MTW GmbH, Wismar, Germany, 2010
63,039g, 240 x 32 m / Twin screw / 22 knots
1,200 pass. / 85 crew
230 cars / 5,500 lane metres

Making good time™

STENA HOLLANDICA
HOEK VAN HOLLAND

Stena Britannica - 2010

Wadan Yards MTW GmbH, Wismar, Germany, 2010
63,600g, 240 x 32 m / Twin screw / 22 knots
1,200 pass. / 85 crew
230 cars / 5,500 lane metres

The second ship in the series of new tonnage for Harwich–Hoek van Holland service, she entered commercial service in October 2010. The Stena Britannica and her sister ship the Stena Hollandica are two of the largest Superferries in the world.

Stena Scotia - 2011

Miho Shipyard, Shimizu, China, 1996
13,017g / 142.5 x 23.2 m / Twin screw / 18 knots
12 pass. / 1,562 lane metres

Built in 1996 for Norfolk Line as Maersk Exporter, this freight ferry was renamed Scotia Seaways in 2010 when DFDS acquired Norfolk Line. Shortly afterwards she was sold to Stena Line and renamed Stena Scotia. In 2020 the ship was operating on the Heysham–Belfast link.

Stena Feronia - 2011

Cantiere Navale Visentini Francesco & C., Donada, Italy, 1997
21,856g / 186 x 26 m / Twin screw / 24 knots
340 pass. / 100 cars / 2,460 lane metres
Stena service: 2011-2015

Built as the Mersey Viking for charter to Norse Irish Ferries. Entered service in July 1997 between Liverpool and Belfast. Later sold DFDS and then to Stena Line in February 2011 and renamed Stena Feronia. Sold to Strait Shipping, New Zealand in 2015 and renamed Strait Feronia.

Stena Hibernia - 2011

Miho Shipyard, Shimizu, China, 1996
13,017g / 142.5 x 23.5 m / Twin screw / 18 knots
12 pass. / 1,562 lane metres

Built in 1996 for Norfolk Line as Maersk Importer and a sister to Stena Scotia, she was renamed Hibernia Seaways in 2010 following the takeover of the company by DFDS. A few months later she was purchased by Stena Line and renamed Stena Hibernia. Like her sister the vessel was operating on the Heysham-Belfast link in 2020.

Stena Transporter - 2011

Samsung Heavy Industries Co Ltd, Geoje Shipyard, South Korea, 2011
33,690g / 212 x 26.7 m / Twin screw / 22 knots
300 pass. / 4,057 lane metres

Built in South Korea for the 11-hour crossing between Killingholme-Hoek van Holland route, the Stena Transporter entered service in March 2011.

Stena Transit - 2011

Samsung Heavy Industries Co Ltd, Geoje Shipyard, South Korea, 2011
33,690g / 212 x 26.7 m / Twin screw / 22 knots
300 pass. / 4,000 lane metres

Sister to the Stena Transporter, the Stena Transit is operating on the Killingholme–Hoek van Holland link. Like her sister, she was fitted with a scrubber unit during 2015.

Stena Lagan - 2012

Cantiere Navale Visentini Francesco & C., Donada, Italy, 2005
26,500g / 186.5 x 25.6 m / Twin screw / 24 knots
480 pass. / 170 cars / 2,275 lane metres

Entering service in March 2006 as the Lagan Viking, the vessel was later named Lagan Seaways with DFDS. She was renamed Stena Lagan in 2011, then purchased by Stena Line in 2012. Both the 'Lagan' and her sister where lengthened during 2020/21 in Turkey for their new role in the Baltic operations as from 2021.

Stena Mersey - 2012

Cantiere Navale Visentini Francesco & C., Donada, Italy, 2005
27,510g / 186.5 x 25.6 m / Twin screw / 24 knots
480 pass. / 170 cars / 2,275 lane metres

Built by Visentini in Italy for the charter market initially but later chartered during construction to Norse Irish Ferries, becoming the Mersey Viking. Later named Mersey Seaways under DFDS and then Stena Mersey. Acquired by Stena in 2012.

Sassnitz - 2012

Danyard A/S, Aalborg, Denmark, 1989
20,276g, 171.5 x 24 m / Twin screw / 20 knots
900 pass. / 220 cars / 56 railway wagons / 711 lane metres

Built as a train/roro ferry for the Sassnitz–Trelleborg route and later put on the Trelleborg–Rostock operation. Acquired by Stena Line in 2012 and later put on the Sassnitz–Trelleborg service. Withdrawn from service in March 2020 during the Covid-19 pandemic.

Stena Flavia - 2012 (chartered)

Cantiere Navale Visentini Francesco & C., Porto Viro, Italy, 2009
26,904g / 186.4 x 25.6 m / Twin screw / 24 knots
800 pass. / 195 cars / 2,255 lane metres

Built by Visentini in Italy as the Watling Street. After service in the Mediterranean she moved to the Baltic before she was purchased by Stena Line and renamed Stena Flavia for further service in that area and a short period on the Rosslare–Cherbourg link.

Mecklenburg-Vorpommern - 2012

Schichau Seebeckswerft, Bremerhaven, Germany, 1996
37,987g / 199.9 x 28.9 m / Twin screw / 21 knots
600 pass. / 90 railway wagons / 3,200 lane metres

Built as train ferry/roro vessel for the Rostock–Trelleborg. Acquired by Stena Line in 2012 and remains on the route she has served on since 1996.

Scottish Viking - 2012 (chartered)

Cantiere Navale Visentini Francesco & C., Porto Viro, Italy, 2009
26,904g / 186 x 25.6 m / Twin screw / 24 knots
800 pass. / 195 cars / 2,250 lane metres

Placed on the Zeebrugge–Rosyth freight service of DFDS after construction in Italy. After her charter to DFDS she was chartered by Scandlines and then later by Stena Line in 2012 for the Ventspils–Nynäshamn service.

Urd - 2013

Nuovi Cantieri Apuania S.p.A, Marina di Carrara, Italy, 1981
11,030g / 176 x 23.5 m / Twin screw / 17.5 knots
600 pass. / 325 cars / 1,600 lane metres

Built as the Easy Rider, operated initially in the Mediterranean before her sale to Sealink. Renamed the Seafreight Highway for operations at Dover and Holyhead. In 1988 returned to the Mediterranean. In 1997 sold to Scandlines. After re-sale in 2013 she was chartered long-term to Stena Line for their operations in the Baltic.

Stena Baltica - 2013 (chartered)

Aker Finnyards, Helsinki, Finland, 2007
22,308g / 167.8 x 26.8 m / Twin screw / 23 knots
213 pass. / 2,188 lane metres

Built for Brittany Ferries as the Cotentin for the freight services between Cherbourg–Poole/Poole–Santander. In 2013 chartered to Stena Line and renamed the Stena Baltica for service on the Gdynia–Karlskrona route.

Stena Alegra - 2013

Astilleros Españoles, Sevilla, Spain, 1998
22,152g / 179.9 x 25.3 m / Twin screw / 24 knots
195 pass. / 2,000 lane metres
Stena service: 2011, 2013-2015

Built as a series five ships, the Dawn Merchant entered service on the Irish Sea in 1999. After charter work in the Mediterranean, English Channel and Irish Sea she was sold to Stena Line 2013 and renamed the Stena Alegra. Later chartered to Interislander, New Zealand and renamed the Kaiarahi.

Stena Horizon - 2014 (chartered)

Cantiere Navale Visentini Francesco & C., Donada, Italy, 2006
26,500g / 186.5 x 25.6 m / Twin screw / 24 knots
1,000 pass. / 170 cars / 2,270 lane metres

Built at Visentini in Italy as the Cartour Beta in a series of seventeen freight vessels. After service in the Mediterranean she was chartered to Celtic Link and renamed the Celtic Horizon. In 2014 Stena Line acquired the route between Cherbourg and Rosslare and renamed her the Stena Horizon.

Stena Superfast X – 2015

The *Superfast X* entered service for Superfast Ferries in February 2002 on the Hanko–Rostock route, and later in the year she was put on the Rosyth–Zeebrugge route. Following the closure of the Scottish service the *Superfast X* was rebuilt in Norway with additional passenger berths. In 2006, Superfast Ferries announced they had sold the *Superfast X* to Veolia Transport for €112 million and the ship was renamed the *Jean Nicoli* for service in the Mediterranean.

Four years later SeaFrance acquired her and renamed the former Greek

ship the *SeaFrance Molière*. With the demise of SeaFrance operations during 2012, DFDS chartered the ship for their operations on the Dover Strait as *Dieppe Seaways*. At the end of her charter to DFDS Seaways in November 2014, Stena Line acquired the ship and renamed her the *Stena Superfast X*; she underwent an extensive refit including improvements to her freight decks and refurbishment of her interior on a similar line to her near sisterships *Stena Superfast VII* and *Stena Superfast VIII*. After refit she replaced the *Stena Nordica* on the Holyhead–Dublin Port route as from March 2015.

The *Stena Superfast X* substantially increased the freight and passenger capacity on the route and coincided with the withdrawal of the Stena HSS service to Dun Laoghaire.

Following the delivery of the first 'E Flexer' ship at Holyhead in late 2019, Stena Line announced that *Stena Superfast X* had been chartered to Corsica Linea and was renamed *A Nepita*.

Howaldtswerke Deutsche Werft AG, Kiel, Germany, 2002
30,285g / 203.9 x 25.4 m / Twin screw / 28.9 knots
1,200 pass. / 661 cars / 1,891 lane metres

STENA SUPERFAST X
CARDIFF

Stena Superfast VII - 2017

Howaldtswerke Deutsche Werft AG, Kiel, Germany, 2001
30,285g / 203.9 x 25 m / Twin screw / 28.9 knots
1,200 pass. / 661 cars / 1,891 lane metres

Ordered by Superfast for the Rostock–Hanko link. In 2006 she was sold to Tallink for their Helsinki–Rostock link. In 2011 she was chartered to Stena Line for their new service between Belfast and Cairnryan and renamed Stena Superfast VII. In 2017 Stena Line purchased her.

Finnclipper - 2017 (chartered)

Astilleros Españoles, Puerta Real, Spain, 1999
33,958g / 188.3 x 29.3 m / Twin screw / 22 knots
440 pass. / 3,079 lane metres

Ordered by Stena Line as a series of four RoPax ships and later sold to Finnlines. After various operations in the Baltic up to 2017 she was chartered out to Balearia Group for service between Barcelona and Palma de Mallorca as the Rosalind Franklin.

Stena Superfast VIII - 2017

Howaldtswerke Deutsche Werft AG, Kiel, Germany, 2001
30,285g / 203.3 x 25.4 m / Twin screw / 28.9 knots
1,200 pass. / 661 cars / 1,891 lane metres

Sister to the Stena Superfast VII. Following her being chartered to Stena Line both sister ships underwent major overhaul of their passenger areas including the removal of the majority of their cabins and improvements to their freight decks to accommodate more lorries on the North Channel service. In 2017 the Stena Superfast VIII was purchased by Stena Line.

Elisabeth Russ - 2017 (chartered)

J.J. Sietas, Hamburg, Germany, 1999
10,471g / 153.4 x 20.6 m / 12 pass. / 1,624 lane m.
Stena Line service: 2017-2018

On delivery the Elisabeth Russ was chartered out to Transfennica and placed on the Hanko–Lübeck route. In 2017 she was chartered to Stena Line for their Gdynia–Nynäshamn operations for six months.

Stena Forerunner - 2018

Dalian Shipyard, Dalian, China, 2003
24,688g / 195.3 x 26.8 m / Twin screw / 22.5 knots
12 pass. / 3,000 lane metres

Ordered by Stena Line in a series of three sister ships from China. Carried various charter work up until 2018 when placed on the North Sea and Irish Sea operations as relief and back-up vessel. In 2020 operating Harwich–Rotterdam freight service.

Mistral - 2018 (chartered)

J.J. Sietas KG Schiffswerft GmbH , Hamburg, Germany, 1998
10,471g / 153.4 x 20.6 m / Single screw / 22 knots
12 pass. / 1,625 lane metres

Built for Godby Shipping, Finland. Chartered out for five years to Transfennica on delivery for service between Hanko–Lübeck. In 2018 the vessel was chartered to Stena Line for the Rotterdam–Harwich link.

Stena Vinga - 2018

Merwede Werft BV, Hardinxveld-Giessendam, Holland, 2005
14,551g / 129.9 x 23.4 m / Twin screw / 18.5 knots
400 pass. / 1,500 lane metres

Built as the Hammerodde for the Køge–Rønne–Ystad service of Bornholmslinjen. In 2017 she was sold to Stena Line and renamed Stena Vinga as a back up ferry on the Frederikshavn–Gothenburg route and for relief operations in the fleet.

Stena Forecaster - 2019

Dalian Shipyard, Dalian, China, 2003
24,688g / 195.3 x 26.8 m / Twin screw / 22.5 knots
12 pass. / 3,000 lane metres

A sister to the Stena Forerunner, she was chartered out to Transfennica on delivery for their Hanko–Lübeck link. In 2019 the Stena Forecaster was deployed on the Birkenhead–Belfast route, pending the arrival of the new 'E Flexer' vessels for the route.

Stena Estrid - 2019

The E-Flexer class of Ro-Pax ferries were ordered by Stena RoRo for European ferry operations, either for their own operations or for charter. Nine vessels in the class have now been ordered from China, with the last two in the series been slightly larger in the hull configurations.

Following around two years of design work, Stena ordered the first four vessels of the class initially for their Irish Sea services. In the event the first vessel the *Stena Estrid* replaced the *Stena Superfast X* to increase capacity on the Central Corridor and second and fourth ship were placed on the Birkenhead-Belfast link,

meanwhile the third ship in the series was chartered to Brittany Ferries.

In February 2018, the keel was laid for the *Stena Estrid*, with her delivery scheduled late 2019. Meanwhile Stena RoRo ordered a fifth ship in April 2018 for DFDS Seaways, the following month they ordered a sixth ship for charter to Brittany Ferries, with an additional ship later secured for the French company.

Launched in January 2019, the *Stena Estrid*, was delivered in November to the Swedish company. She made her maiden voyage on 13 January 2020 between Holyhead and Dublin and will

operate in the long-term with the *Stena Adventurer*. At 215 metres in length, the *Stena Estrid* now offers a deck space of 3,100 lane meters, an increase of more than 50 % in freight capacity compared to her predecessor the *Stena Superfast X*. In addition, she has a separate car deck, like all the sisters in the series, allowing all main decks to be dedicated to freight traffic.

AVIC Weihai Shipyard, Weihai, China, 2019
41,671g / 214.5 x 28.4 m / Twin screw / 22 knots
1,000 pass. / 120 cars / 3,100 lane metres

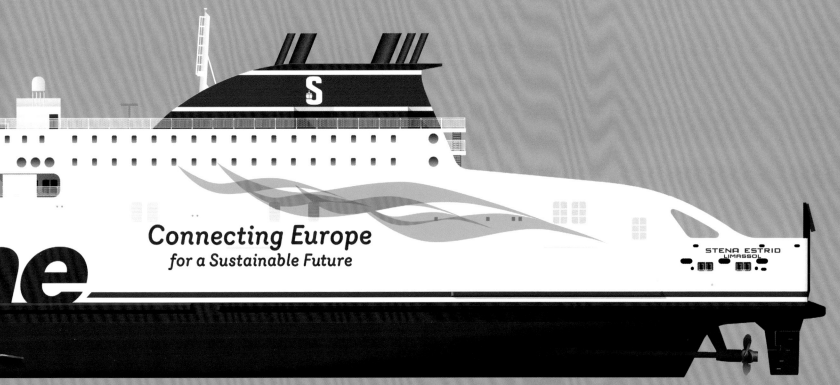

Stena Edda - 2020

AVIC Weihai Shipyard, Weihai, China, 2020
41,671g / 214.5 x 27.8 m / Twin screw / 22 knots
1,000 pass. / 120 cars / 3,100 lane metres

The Stena Edda, the second 'E-Flexer' earmarked for Birkenhead–Belfast link, was delivered to Stena Line on 15 January 2020. Following her 10,000-mile voyage via Singapore and Gibraltar, she entered service on Stena's route between Belfast and Liverpool on 9 March 2020, allowing the Stena Lagan to go for jumboization.

Stena Embla - 2021

AVIC Weihai Shipyard, Weihai, China, 2020
41,671g / 214.5 x 27.8 m / Twin screw / 22 knots
1,000 pass. / 120 cars / 3,100 lane metres

Following completion of her sea trials in October 2020, the Stena Embla was officially handed over and she set sail in late autumn to Belfast, in time to start operating on the Belfast to Birkenhead route in early 2021 alongside sister ship Stena Edda. She is replacing the Stena Mersey, which has successfully operated on the Belfast to Birkenhead route for 10 years.

Top and middle: Interior views of the Stena Estrid.

Bottom: The third E Flexer was chartered to Brittany Ferries. The Galicia arrives at Portsmouth prior to handover to the French company.

Stena Estrid *on sea trials.*

A selection of other ships chartered by Stena Line

Seute Deern - 1963

Rheinstahl Nordseewerke, Emden, Germany, 1963
769g / 57.5 x 10.1 m / 600 pass.
Stena Line service: 1963

This charming little ship was briefly used by Stena Line in 1963 on the Göteborg–Skagen route, otherwise spending her entire career on the Helgoland service from Hamburg. Seute Deern was withdrawn in 2003 and went to a static role in Hamburg harbour.

Hein Godewind - 1964

J.J. Sietas, Hamburg, Germany, 1963
980g / 59.6 x 11.1 m / 825 pass.
Stena Line service: 1964

Usually operating the Cuxhaven–Helgoland route, the Hein Godewind was chartered by Stena for 6 months in 1964 and placed on the Faaborg–Kiel route. She was sold in 2001 and was to be transformed into a private yacht, but she remained laid up at Gibraltar where she eventually sank on 21 December 2007.

Prinsessan Christina - 1966

Aalborg Skibsværft A/S, Ålborg, Denmark, 1960
2,240g / 86.5 x 14.8 m / 809 pass. / 152 cars
Stena Line service: 1966

Ordered by Sessan Line for the Fredrikshavn–Göteborg route, the Prinsessan Christina was chartered for 7 months to Stena Line in 1966 and placed on their 'Londoner' Channel service from Tilbury to Calais.

Völkerfreundschaft - 1966

Götaverken, Göteborg, Sweden, 1948
12,165g / 160.1 x 21 m / 390 pass.
Stena Line service: 1966-1985

Built in 1948 as the Stockholm for the Swedish–America Line, this transatlantic liner is best known for colliding with the Andrea Doria off the coast of Nantucket on 25 July 1956, resulting in the italian ship being sunk. In 1960 she was sold to East Germany and renamed Völkerfreundschaft. From 1966 to 1985, she was chartered to Stena Line every winter for Caribbean cruises from Göteborg. Totally rebuilt in 1993, this ship lives on today as the Astoria.

Viking II - 1971 (Earl William - 1990)

Kaldnes Mekaniske Verksted A/S, Tönsberg, Norway, 1964
3,670g / 99.5 x 18.3 m / 940 pass. / 180 cars
Stena Line service: 1971 / 1990-1991

Originally built in 1964 for Thoresen Car Ferries as the Viking II, she was briefly chartered to Stena in 1971. Sold to Sealink in 1976 and renamed the Earl William. she was used again by Stena in the early 1990s.

Skagen - 1973

Pusnes Mekaniske Verksted / Kristiansands Mekaniske Verksted, Norway, 1958
1,870g / 80.7 x 13.8 m / 505 pass. / 75 cars
Stena Line service: 1973

Operating on the Skagerrak Straits between Norway and Denmark for A/S Kristiansands Dampskibsselskap, the Skagen was purchased by Fred. Olsen in 1968. In 1973 she was used by Stena for 3 months on their Korsör–Kiel route.

Viking Victory - 1976

Kaldnes Mekaniske Verksted A/S, Tönsberg, Norway, 1964
3,680g / 99.5 x 18.3 m / 940 pass. / 180 cars
Stena Line service: 1976

One of the most revolutionary car ferries to operate from the UK, the Viking I opened Thoresen's Western English Channel routes in 1964. In 1976 she was renamed Viking Victory and chartered by Stena Line to operate the Göteborg–Frederikshavn route for 3 months.

Scandinavica - 1978

Dubigeon Normandie S.A., Nantes, France, 1973
11,344g / 141.5 x 19.9 m / 975 pass. / 270 cars
Stena Line service: 1978-1981

A sister to the Massalia (see page 45), the Bolero spent most of her time on charter for Prince Of Fundy Line in summer and cruising for Commodore Cruise Lines in winter. From 1978 to 1981 Stena Line operated her as the Scandinavica on the Göteborg–Kiel service and occasional cruising from Göteborg.

Dana Sirena - 1978

Cantieri Navali Riuniti del Tirreno, Riva Trigoso, Italy, 1969
7,697g / 124.9 x 19.3 m / 718 pass. / 120 cars
Stena Line service: 1978

Initially operating the Copenhagen–Ålborg run for DFDS as the Aalborghus and renamed Dana Sirena in 1971 for the Genoa–Palma de Mallorca–Malaga–Alicante–Patras service, she was briefly used by Stena Line in January-February 1978 on the Göteborg–Kiel route.

Saint Patrick II - 1985

J.J. Sietas, Hamburg, Germany, 1973
7,984g / 125.2 x 21.5 m / 1,612 pass. / 300 cars
Stena Line service: 1985-1986

The former Aurella of Viking Line was purchased in 1982 by Irish Ferries and renamed Saint Patrick II, operating the Rosslare–Le Havre / Cherbourg service. She was chartered by Stena Line during the winter season 1985-86 on the Moss–Fredrikshavn–Göteborg route.

Norröna - 1994

Werft Nobiskrug Rendsburg, Germany, 1973
12,159g / 128.8 x 20.8 m / 1,040 pass. / 250 cars
Stena Line service: 1994-1995

The Gustav Vasa of Lion Ferry was sold to Smyril Line in 1983. Renamed Norröna and fitted with stabilisers she sailed their Denmark-Faroe Islands-Iceland route. From January to March 1994 she was chartered by Stena Sealink on the Fishguard–Rosslare and Holyhead–Dun Laoghaire routes, then again in 1995 between Stranraer and Larne.

Rosebay - 1994

J.J. Sietas, Hamburg, Germany, 1976
5,631g / 135.5 x 21.7 m / 63 pass. / 1,624 lane m.
Stena Line service: 1994-1997, 1998-2001

Originally the Transgermania, the Rosebay was first chartered by Stena from 1994 to 1997 to serve on the Rotterdam/Hook Of Holland–Harwich route, then again from 1998 to 2001 on various Channel routes.

Greifswald - 1999

VEB Mathias Thesen Werft, Wismar, East Germany, 1988
20,084g / 190.9 x 26 m / 12 pass. / 1,570 lane m.
Stena service: 1999

From January to March 1999 this former train ferry was chartered by Stena to operate between Göteborg and Kiel while the route's regular ferries Stena Germanica and Stena Scandinavica were being upgraded.

Stena Challenger - 2005

Van der Giessen De Noord, Krimpen an de Ijssel, Holland, 1995
22,365g / 181.6 x 23.4 m / 1,650 pass. / 600 cars
Stena service: 2005

In 2005 the ex-Isle Of Innisfree, Pride Of Cherbourg was chartered for 6 months by Stena Line to operate between Karlskrona and Gdynia. She later became the Kaitaki on the 'Interislander' route between Picton and Wellington.

Stena Marstrandica - 2015

Lunde Varv & Mekaniska Verkstad Ab, Ramvik, Sweden, 1984
94g / 23 x 8 m / 329 pass.
Stena service: 2015

Operated by the municipality of Kungälv between Koön and Martstrandsön, the double-ended ferry Lasse Maja III was chartered to Stena Line for just one week in Summer 2015 during the Stena Match Cup sailing competition in Marstrand and renamed Stena Marstrandica for the occasion.

Bore Bay - 2018

Umoe Sterkoder A.S, Kristiansund, Norway, 1996
19,094g / 138.5 x 22.7 m / 12 pass. / 1,511 lane m.
Stena service: 2018-2019

The 1996-built ro-ro freight ferry Heralden was converted in 2007 into the car carrier Auto Bay for UECC, only to be reconverted back to ro-ro freighter ten years later and renamed Bore Bay. From April 2018 she was chartered by Stena Line to replace the Elisabeth Russ on the thrice-weekly Gdynia–Nynäshamn Stena route.

Vikingland - 2018

Rauma Repola OY, Rauma, Finland, 1982
20,381g / 155 x 25.2 m / 12 pass. / 2,160 lane m.
Stena Line service: 2018-2019

In August 2018 the Vikingland (ex-Aurora) replaced the Bore Bay on the Gdynia–Nynäshamn route, adding 30% freight capacity.

Somerset - 2018

Flender Werft, Lübeck, Germany, 2000
21,005g / 138.4 x 25.2 m / 12 pass. / 2,475 lane m.

Built in Germany as the Spaarneborg, this freight ferry is under a 3-year charter for Stena Line, operating the Europoort–Harwich route.

Seatruck Panorama - 2020

Astilleros de Sevilla, Huelva, Spain, 2008
14,759g / 142 x 23 m / 12 pass. / 1,830 lane m.

From September 2020 this ro-ro freight ferry is operating services from Belfast to Birkenhead and Heysham.

An oddity: Stefan - 1990

Lauched as the *Maasdam* for Holland America Line in 1952, this mid-sized transatlantic liner was designed as a 90 percent tourist-class ship, with only 39 first class berths arranged in an exclusive penthouse section on the upper decks.

Originally operating the Bremerhaven-New York service, the *Maasdam* was transferred to the Rotterdam-Montréal route in 1966.

Sold to Polish Ocean Lines in 1968 and renamed the *Stefan Batory,* she started maintaining their regular service between Gdynia, Rotterdam, Southampton and Montreal the following year. The comfortable little liner quickly proved to be great success, mostly because there was no direct air link between Poland and the New World at that time, but also because she offered a simple and economical alternative to cross the Atlantic compared to luxury superliners such as the *France* and *Queen Elizabeth 2*. Additionally, she was a welcome source of foreign currency for Poland at the time.

Decommissioned in 1988, the *Stefan Batory* was purchased by Stena in 1989 on behalf of the Swedish government to operate as an accommodation ship for refugees in Göteborg as the *Stefan*. In 1991 she was laid up in Greece and remained idle until being sent to Turkey for scrapping in 2000.

Wilton-Fijenoord Shipyard, Schiedam, Holland, 1952
15,024g / 153.4 x 21.1 m / Single screw / 15.6 knots / 861 pass. / 336 crew
Stena Line service: 1990-1991

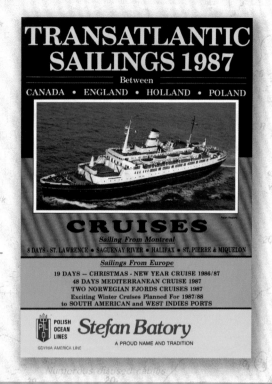

TRANSATLANTIC SAILINGS 1987
Between
CANADA • ENGLAND • HOLLAND • POLAND

CRUISES
Sailing From Montreal
8 DAYS - ST. LAWRENCE • SAGUENAY RIVER • HALIFAX • ST. PIERRE & MIQUELON

Sailings From Europe
19 DAYS — CHRISTMAS - NEW YEAR CRUISE 1986/87
48 DAYS MEDITERRANEAN CRUISE 1987
TWO NORWEGIAN FJORDS CRUISES 1987
Exciting Winter Cruises Planned For 1987/88
to SOUTH AMERICAN and WEST INDIES PORTS

POLISH OCEAN LINES — *Stefan Batory*
GDYNIA AMERICA LINE — A PROUD NAME AND TRADITION

Evolution of the Stena Line livery

1964

1972

1981

1996

2010

2019

Stena Line scrapbook of old ships in new waters

Below: After her operations on the Irish Sea the Stena Normandica was sold in 1990 to Moby Lines becoming the Moby Vincent for service on the Livorno–Bastia link.

Above: The third Stena Nordica of 1975 was sold to RMT for their Ostend-Dover service and became the Reine Astrid in 1983. In 1997 she was sold to Moby Lines and then chartered to Comanav for the Algeciras–Tangier service as the Al Mansour.

After service in Canada as the Marine Nautica, the former Stena Line ship saw service with Corsica Ferries. She is pictured here as the Corsica Marina Seconda.

Above: The much travelled 1974-built Stena Nordica *is seen here leaving Calais as the* SeaFrance Monet *in 1997. After her service on the English Channel she moved to Canary Islands for final years of operations until 2005 .*

Above: A powerful view of the 1967-built Stena Britannica *pictured as the* Sardegna Bella *whilst operating on the Livorno–Olbia service. She remained in service until 1998.*

Above: The former Stena Scandinavica *of 1973 was sold to Irish Ferries in 1978. This view shows her as the* Saint Killian II *leaving Rosslare during her final season with the company.*

Above: The Ialyssos, *ex-Finnpartner,* Stena Baltica *(1978), makes an early morning arrival at Piraeus in September 1996.*

Right: Built in 1973 as the Stena Jutlandica, *the former Swedish ferry is seen leaving Algeciras for Tangier as the* Euroferries Atlantica.

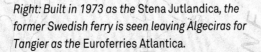

Below: In 2013 the Stena Caledonia was withdrawn from service and sold to Indonesia, becoming the Port Link for service between Merak and Bakauheni.

Above: After her sale by Stena Line in 1999 the former Stena Cambria saw service on a number of operations in Mediterranean. In 2020 she remains in service as the Bari.

Right: The former Stena Galloway arrives at Algeciras as the Morocco Sun. She has been very close to being scrapped a number of times but following an extensive refit in 2016 it appears that her career has been extended.

Below: Built as the Prinsessan Birgitta the former Sessan ship was sold to Irish Ferries in 1999. She remained with the company for eight years on the Cherbourg and Roscoff operations.

Above: The St Columba/Stena Hibernia was sold in 1997 for further service in Greece. In 2006 in light of new fast craft tonnage she was sold as a pilgrim ship. She seen here as the Masarrah in the Red Sea.

Above: Built as the Stena Traveller, in 2020 she operates on the Paldiski–Kapellskär/Paldiski–Hanko link for DFDS as the Patria Seaways.

Above: Built as the Stena Challenger the former Stena Line ship now operates as the Leif Ericson between North Sydney and Port Aux Basques / Argentia in Canada.

Below: The much travelled Superfast X was chartered out by Stena Line in 1999 to Corsica Linea. She is seen here shortly after entering service in the Mediterranean as the A Nepita.

Above: Sadly, following her withdrawal from service the Stena Baltica has never fitted in long-term on any route in the Mediterranean. The former Crown Line ship is seen here at Naples as the SNAV Adriatico.

Above: In 2020 the former Stena Felicity operates for Ventouris Ferries as the Rigel II.

Fleet Index

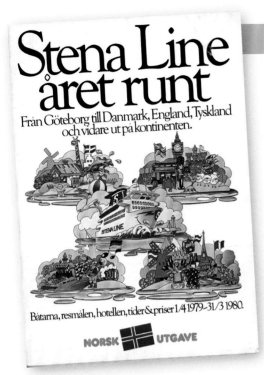

Stena Line året runt

Från Göteborg till Danmark, England, Tyskland och vidare ut på kontinenten.

Båtarna, resmålen, hotellen, tider & priser 1/4 1979-31/3 1980.

NORSK UTGAVE

Fleet Index

Stena Precision.

Acknowledgements

The authors would like to thank John Bryant for writing the Introduction to the book and also for checking the publication. Thanks also goes to Richard Seville for allowing us to use the drawing of the *Stena Horsa*. A final word of thanks goes to Bruce Peter who has assisted us with so many historical images for this publication.

Bibliography, reference books & websites

- *Stena Line- The story of a ferry company* by Klas Brogren – Stena Line/Ship Pax
- *Stena Line - Celebrating 50 years of service* by Bruce Peter – Ferry Publications
- *In Waters New* by Richard Seville – Ferry Publications
- *Ferry & Cruise Review Magazine* published by Ferry Publications 1989 – 2020
- http://www.faktaomfartyg.se
- https://blog.stenaline.com

Source of illustrations & photographic credits

Marc-Antoine Bombail: All ship illustrations, except page 28 (Stena RoRo).

Wolfgang Bamitzke/fleetmon.com: 58 (bottom).

John Bryant: 52 (top R), 53 (top L), 59 (bottom L), 82 (bottom R), 85 (col 3 bottom), 86 (col 3 middle), 92 (col 1 top, col 2 bottom).

Rob de Visser: 70, 72 (top L, bottom R), 79 (top L).

FotoFlite: 2, 17, 34 (top L, bottom L), 65 (top L), 85 (col 1 top).

Frank Heine: 90 (top L).

Gordon Hislip: 29, 59 (top R, bottom R), 61 (top L+R), 68 (top R, bottom L), 73 (top R, bottom L+R).

Darren Holdaway: 76, 86 (col 3 bottom).

Andy Kilk: 45 (bottom L).

Frank Lose: 24, 43 (bottom), 47 (top R), 51 (bottom R), 52 (bottom R), 48, 65 (bottom L, top R), 72 (bottom R), 75 (bottom R), 93 (col 1 middle).

Mike Louagie: 91 (col 1 top).

Matt Murtland: 75 (top R).

Bruce Peter collection: 16, 23, 34 (R), 39 (top R), 40 (bottom L & R, top R), 41, 44 (bottom L, top R), 47 (bottom), 50 (top L, bottom), 51 (top L+R, bottom L), 52 (top L), 63 (bottom R), 64 (bottom L+R), 65 (top R, bottom L+R), 66, 68 (bottom L), 69 (top R, bottom L+R), 74 (top L, bottom L+R), 75 (bottom L), 78 (top L, bottom L), 85 (col 1 bottom L, col 2), 90 (bottom), 93 (col 1 bottom, col 1 top).

Stena Line: 22 (bottom), 26, 27, 28, 67 (bottom), 75 (top L), 78 (bottom R), 80, 81, 82 (all except bottom R), 83, 86 (col 2 top).

Stena Line Archives: 2, 3, 4, 5 (top), 6, 8, 9, 13, 14, 35, 39 (top L), 42 (top L), 43 (top), 96.

Stena RoRo: 7.

Wikimedia Commons: 37 (top L), 50 (top R), 59 (bottom R), 61 (top R), 74 (top R), 78 (top R), 79 (bottom R), 84 (col 1).

All other pictures by Miles Cowsill or from the Ferry Publications Library.

Entering the first Stena Germanica...